Following the Silence

In loving memory of
my husband, Don

and also

To my dear Sisters of the Love of God, Oxford

Following the Silence

A Contemplative Journey

Georgina Alexander

GRACEWING

First published in 2009

Gracewing
2 Southern Avenue
Leominster
Herefordshire HR6 0QF

ISBN 978 0 85244 492 4

Illustrations by Glenn Shipton
(based on an idea of Georgina Alexander)

Typeset by Action Publishing Technology Ltd
Gloucester GL1 5SR

Contents

Acknowledgements   vii
Foreword ix
Preface xi
A Note on the Illustrations xv

Part One

1. The Call Deepens 3
2. The Cloister Within 11
3. Further Steps on the Way 17
4. Finding the Door, 1973 21
5. Descent to Contrition 25
6. Moving On 29

Part Two

7. Energies 35
8. A Healing Ministry 43
9. Inner Healing – The Holy Spirit 47
10. The Purpose of the Christian Life 51
11. Emptiness 55

Part Three

Reflections on the Night	63
We go to God from Light into Darkness	63
Growing into a Likeness of Christ	77
Intercession	79
A Hermit in Community	84
Suggested Readings	87

Acknowledgements

I acknowledge with deepest gratitude the encouragement of Fr Donald Allchin [Canon Arthur McDonald Allchin], who urged me to read and study, as well as to pray; and Dr Martin Groves, head of Theology, Religion and Culture at Oxford Brookes University, who suggested that I write in a narrative mode. I also thank Fr Seraphim Vanttinen-Newton of the Annunciation Orthodox Church in Oxford, for his support and advice.

Many thanks also for the generous welcome and fellowship I have received from the congregation of St James the Great at Hanslope, Buckinghamshire, and the Vicar, Fr Gary Ecclestone, SSC.

I also thank and appreciate the support I have had from Tom Longford, Managing Director of Gracewing, and Sr Mary Joseph McManamon, OSB, the patient editor he assigned to help me.

Note

Psalms are taken from the *American Prayer Book, Anglican version*. Other scripture quotes are taken from the Revised Standard Version of the Bible, unless otherwise indicated.

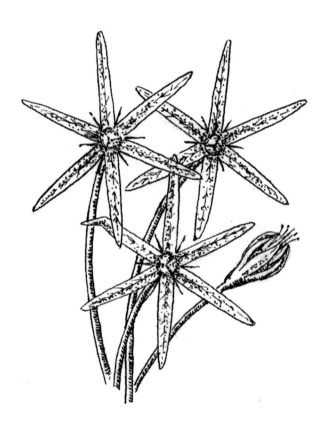

Foreword

Today's religious world shows great interest in meditation. Many people spend fifteen or twenty minutes morning and evening quietly reciting 'the Jesus Prayer' or some sacred word like 'Maranatha'. Perhaps there is an evolution in consciousness whereby larger numbers are called to contemplation.

When people meditate in this way for several years, they may move into a new state of consciousness. This may take the form of a deep silence in which they are unable to pray and unable to think. It may be that they see things and people in a new way. Or the dark side of their personality may come to the surface. Or their life may become stormy. Or the time may come when a new energy arises in the depth of their being. In these circumstances people look for guidance.

Meditators will find sound advice and guidance in the work of Georgina Alexander. She has read the mystics of the Byzantine school, but her work is primarily a description of her own experience and her own search. From an early age she was overtaken with the conviction that Jesus was present within her and she became conscious of a deep still place beyond thoughts and images and feeling. She knows what the mystics call 'the dark night of the soul' and for several years she was unable to pray, overcome with uncertainty, doubt, distress and spiritual ache. But she came to see that this darkness was leading to balance, integrity and fullness of being. Eventually Georgina's path became one of emptiness. 'God cannot help but pour himself into a soul that makes itself

empty before him,' she quotes. And then comes the experience of what the Orthodox mystics call 'uncreated energies'.
This is an experience of energy rising up in the depth of one's
being and filling one's mind and heart and body. The mystics
call this an experience of fire and light. The Orthodox mystics
associate it with the Transfiguration of Jesus, as described in
the ninth chapter of Saint Luke and the seventeenth chapter of
Saint Matthew. Energy is a key to the mystical experience of
all religions. In today's world it is associated with the Hindu
Kundalini.

Here in Tokyo I have a prayer group of Japanese who sit
before the Blessed Sacrament in silence for one hour before
attending mass and adjourning to a small room to chat and
drink Japanese green tea. These Japanese are Christians
except for one leader who is a Buddhist and sits splendidly in
the lotus posture. I shared with them Georgina's account and
they at once understood her message. This confirms me in my
conviction that contemplative prayer is the way of the future
in the world and that Georgina's message is somehow
prophetic.

William Johnston, SJ
Tokyo

Preface

I am writing this account of my own journey because I have become aware that there are many people who have both a capacity and a calling to a life of deep prayer in ordinary and seemingly unlikely situations. Sometimes they are hardly aware of it themselves and even when they are they may not find it easy to get confirmation, support and recognition of their vocation. But it is a vocation that can be followed, however difficult it may seem outwardly, because once a call is recognized, grace is always given.

This account is much more than a deeply personal story, though the beginnings are individual and the background is particularly personal. It does, however, follow a pattern that is recognizable in the Christian tradition which goes right back to the early Fathers and Mothers of the Church.

This story has three dimensions. Not only something of a personal autobiography, which would of course be different for everyone, but also the tracing of a vocation to pray. We all have a capacity for relationship with God and those roots of prayer are from a much deeper level than that of seemingly self-chosen consciousness, though we may not always recognize it at first. This account is also a recognition of the tradition of mystical prayer that is in the Bible and in the teaching of the Fathers and Mothers of the Church that has been in the Christian Church for centuries. This tradition is still available for us now, though sadly it is not often taught or recognized very frequently in the Church today.

It has always been very important to me to feel that I was

in that Christian tradition because my own journey began with an encounter with a person whom I recognized as being Christ – first, as a little child, to Jesus Christ of Nazareth, and later to the cosmic Christ who is alive and present to the whole world at all times. I recognize that other religions do also have a living relationship with God, the creator of the Universe, and I deeply respect them for their beliefs but I feel that it is important for me to remain faithful to my own beginnings, which is why I have sought to find affirmation and confirmation through those early teachings and tradition of the Church. We do actually have all that we need to teach and support us on our journey in that ancient tradition of the Christian Church though I know of at least two members of religious communities, both men and both in Roman Catholic communities, who have been heard to say that 'Contemplation is not for ordinary people, people in the world or in the church congregations'. That is probably an indication that they don't know much about it themselves.

I don't think that God knows that contemplation is 'not for ordinary people in the church'. He seems to give his gifts where he will to whomever he will and isn't necessarily a respecter of our own formulaic system of positions and status and categories. He can and does give his gifts and calling wherever he chooses. When I look back, it has been for me a journey that has seemingly been guided by chance and yet all things do seem to have worked together for the good for me. I guess that is because it has been guided by faith in God's providence.

> He who believes in me will live, even though he dies,
> and whoever lives and believes in me will never die.[1]
> You have not chosen me, I have chosen you.[2]

The seeds of my own journey were sown when I was taken to Sunday School at the age of six, I only went a few times because we moved away from the area but at that Evangelical Sunday School, I was taught that 'God so loved the world that he gave his only Son, that whoever believed in him would not die but would have eternal life'.[3] It impressed me very deeply at the time what a wonderful and generous love that must be and I totally accepted it from then on. It is interesting, on looking back, to realize that I was never taught anything about a God of wrath but only of a God of Love.

When, years later, as an adult, I was intuitively searching for an even deeper meaning to life, the impact of God's love came to me and was recognized as being in a Christian format because the framework of that format was already in place in my unconscious. How very important it is to give young children a foundational knowledge of the Christian faith while they are still young enough to take it in at a deep but simple level; a level, which is childlike but not necessarily childish. When, later on, I had the opportunity to become a Sunday School teacher myself I wondered if I would be used to sow a few seeds of faith for young people.

I had married at eighteen and my mother-in-law suggested that I be confirmed in the Church of England so that I could go to church with my husband. The Vicar who prepared me for confirmation talked about prayer and I said that I just talked to Jesus as if he was there in the room with me. He said that I was very lucky to be able to do that. I didn't know what he meant at that time as I quite genuinely thought that was what everyone did.

After we had been married for six years and had two children, my husband changed his job and we moved to a town that happened to be the home of an Anglican religious community. I quickly settled down to live there and went to church in that parish. Whilst my love for my family was never in doubt and at one level I had all that I could have wished for, yet there was still that sense of an unsatisfied and empty space within myself. I had an inarticulate need to find something or someone, bigger than myself to give myself to. It was as if other people were alongside me but not greater than me and I needed to find that 'something' that was 'other', something that was greater than myself and indeed greater than other people. I sensed, in an inarticulate and wordless way that only God was bigger than myself. To me loving is giving and giving is loving and that was what I sought, 'something else'. It seems to me that everyone has this sense of wanting 'something more' although it is not always consciously recognized or verbalized. Many people seek to find satisfaction through personal success, attainment and achievement, and of course this is and can be the basis of a life of active service to the world, to follow an outer call or an active vocation; but some are called to go inward and to learn to fully integrate that inner call into everyday life, into the situation into which God has put them.

Notes

1. Jn 11:25.
2. Jn 15:16.
3. Jn 3:16.

A Note on the Illustrations

A helpful image to express the concept of unity is an Allium flower; the individual florets all have stems, which meet at a single centre. The centre, or meeting point of the flower stems is an analogy for God and all creation in unity; we as individuals are the stems and florets, God is at the centre. On the outermost part of the flower the stems are furthest from the centre, side by side but not connected; but the nearer they get to the centre, the stems are closely joined to each other. There they are united; a single stem unites them all in the one flower.

As we grow closer to God through the practice of prayer and meditation, the closer we come to the Centre and therefore to each other. The problem of feeling isolated from both God and others is overcome in the experience of the meeting at the Centre. This journey into God and the profound meeting with others in the ground of silence is a single movement. Exterior isolation is overcome in interior communion.

This unity also describes the separation yet similarity between different denominations of the church, the difference yet similarity between world faiths and, yet again, the difference between nations. All different yet basically united at their centre in God.

The problem of separation, either within ourselves, between other people, or in larger organisations, is due to being 'self-centred' and not God-centred. As we grow nearer to each other, so we are more able to relate to others, in compassion and empathy; this is because we realize – that is it becomes real to us – that the other person is a reflection of ourselves in their needs. That is not to say that we are all alike, far from it, but at base we are rooted and united in love and compassion.

Special thanks to Glenn Shipton for his beautiful artwork which had added so much to the theme of this book.

Part One

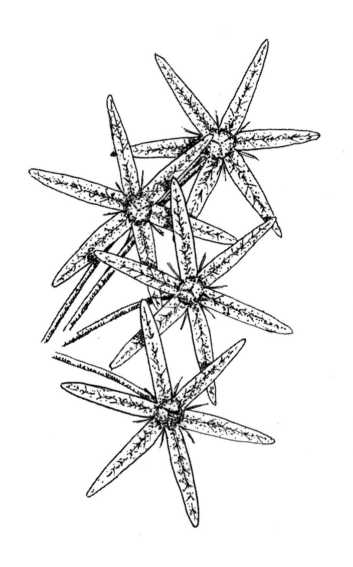

Chapter One

The Call Deepens

You have not chosen me, I have chosen you.[1]
You would not seek me if you had not already found me.
The Kingdom of God is within you.[2]

The call may come in many ways and through many diverse circumstances and is likely to have been founded on earlier experiences of life. In a subconscious way we have been being prepared for it all along though it may be a surprise when it does come.

On one particular occasion I found myself turning back with greater intensity to those childhood memories of relationship with God. As I was going about my work, I was in the kitchen at the time doing the washing up, I was thinking of that empty space; the empty hunger within me, something that needed to be filled, yet knowing that no created thing or person, or state of life could ever fill it.

Over the kitchen sink, I tried to recapture what it would have been like if I had been alive when Jesus was on earth, and I started to ask myself how I would have reacted, what would I have said or done. I said to myself, 'If you, Jesus, were here ...' but no, it should be, 'Now that you *are* here ...' As I asked that question, I was suddenly overwhelmed by the conviction that He was indeed there within me. The power of the experience was amazing; it seemed stunning, almost unbelievable and yet totally and utterly true. When I considered who God is and what He did and to think that He was in me, it seemed quite awe inspiring and almost overwhelming; it took me several days before I settled down again. But from that moment on, it was as if my whole life was turned around in the opposite direction.

> The Most High has wounded me with his Spirit, filled me with his love, and his wounding has become my salvation ...
> All the earth is like a memorial to thee, a presence of thy works. Glory to thee O God, Thou who art for ever the delight of Paradise Alleluia![3]

> Knock, and it shall be opened to you, seek and you will find.[4]

What had been there within me in an unconscious way since childhood now came to the surface and was consciously experienced and realized and I began at once to try to learn how to pray in greater depth so that I could again find Him whom I now knew to be so near. It was the discovery of an invitation to search. 'Seek and you will find, knock and it shall be opened unto you' – that was a text that returned again and again, and underpinned everything that I did. It was indeed a receiving of a 'wound of love' and all that followed thereafter was both caused and led by that wounding.

The parish Sister had called soon after we arrived at our new address, so when I had that first significant sign of a call to prayer I was able to turn to her for advice and support, and she gave me much encouragement. I went up to the local convent and was able to borrow books from their library. The first book I was given to read by that community was *The Imitation of Christ* by Thomas à Kempis and I went on, over the course of many years, to read very widely. When I came upon anything that made reference to other writers, I went back to the source material and soon had collected a good library of my own.

The Sister and I had a very good relationship and after a while I remember saying to her that prayer seemed more like listening than talking; she said that meant that I was called to be a contemplative, though I may not have been fully aware of what that word meant at that time. I was, however, aware of a deep stillness that was beyond words, that stillness was, for me always associated with the presence of Jesus. I needed to be able to listen to the silence and stillness and to ponder and to wait upon it.

It seems that different temperaments pray in different ways and the important thing is to discover what is right for each one of us. No one way is superior to another but it is important for each of us to discover what is our own way and then to be faithful to that pathway, although it is not always clear at the beginning. I believe a lot depends on inner disposition together with having been shaped by outer circumstance, what an educational psychologist would call 'heredity and environment' or, 'nature and nurture'. I read once that God sometimes puts a hermit into the middle of the world and someone with an active temperament into the desert; they both grow more through these seemingly non-conducive circumstances; I am sure that those words related very much to me.

After a while Sister suggested that I go on a retreat at Glastonbury Abbey whilst my mother-in-law came to mind the family. The leader of the retreat was Fr. H. E. W. Slade, a member of the Society of St John the Evangelist, an Anglican community of mission priests. As it was in mid-July, at the time of the Feast of St Mary Magdalen, Father Slade recalled how Mary had told the disciples, 'I have seen Jesus.' I went to him and said that I too had 'seen Jesus'. He was rather disdainful at first and, as most of the people on the retreat were a lot older than me, and I was then only twenty-six, he said I must wait until I was older and more mature. When I explained to him what I meant by 'seeing Jesus' he said he was sorry for being so obtuse.

I asked if I could see him again, and regularly, and he said that I could. 'You will let me say what I think, won't you?' I asked. He agreed but said that he would also say what he thought and would then leave me to obey Jesus or not as I chose. I think he recognized that I had a strong Christ-centred call to prayer but, as I also had a husband and two children to care for, he was, quite rightly, concerned that I did not neglect my outer calling. As I had been confirmed only two days after my wedding day, that really did seem to me to be a sign that God had wanted me to live in the married state of life although it did often seem difficult, if not sometimes almost impossible, to balance the two sides of my calling, but it had to be done and only faith could do it. It seemed that I was called both to be a contemplative and also to learn to integrate that calling into an active state of life, a seemingly impossible task and one that I was to find very demanding.

Father Slade was a great help though he was often very severe, but I always had a sense of confidence in him and he was to guide me for about fifteen years. I greatly valued that relationship which was to be the most influential in my formation, though I probably didn't fully appreciate for many years just how valuable that foundation was and how much I owed him. Although he has long since died, I frequently find myself remembering many of the 'landmark' things he said to me. I had often told him that keeping in balance – balance of the inner and the outer parts of myself: mind, body and spirit – seemed to be essential. I felt then, and I continue to believe, that this is extremely necessary for a stable, grounded life of prayer. Fr Slade was evidently quite relieved to hear me say that. A 'house divided against itself cannot stand'. All through my life I have had the sense that there must be balance and unity among all parts of oneself, and in any times of crisis that was a keystone to be returned to.

> He prays unceasingly who combines prayer with necessary duties and duties with prayer. Only in this way can we find it practicable to fulfil the commandment to pray always. It consists in regarding the whole of Christian existence as a single great prayer. What we are accustomed to call prayer is only part of it.[5]

These words, though written in the second century, are exactly right for someone called to live a life of prayer in the world of today. This reinforces and confirms my belief that the old traditions and teachings are just as relevant to us nowadays as when they were first written many hundreds of years ago. Another thing Fr Slade said, which has always been true, was that I could see further than I had got, in other words, the insights I had had made clear the possibilities for spiritual growth that were before me, even though I could not always live up to them at the time. It was as if I had been to the top of a mountain and seen the promises that lay ahead but then had to go down into the valleys where I could no longer see the view, even though I was in actual fact nearer to my destination.

I went on with my daily life of running the home and caring for my family, taking a few minutes for prayer whenever I had time. St Teresa said, 'If you want to find God waiting at time of prayer, never go far from him at other times.' Because of my desire to pray and again encounter the Jesus I had already met, I tried to train myself to be recollected during the daily round of my life. I used to say words of prayer whilst doing various household chores, such as ironing or washing up, walking up the stairs, walking up to the shops and so on. I continued to do as much Bible and spiritual reading as was possible and I went to communion when I could so I continued to grow in knowledge of the liturgical seasons of the church, though I had always kept up Bible reading since those early days and that had given me a good grounding in the Christian faith.

I used to haunt the second-hand bookshops in the nearby University City of Oxford; and Foyle's of Charing Cross Road had a mail-order business then, which I frequently used. One of the first books I bought for myself was *Holy Wisdom* by Fr Augustine Baker, OSB. I was delighted and greatly affirmed to read that he said that deep prayer was for everyone, not only for priests and monks and nuns, so that meant that there was indeed hope for me. I continued to borrow books from the local convent; one book leading on to another and, whenever I saw a reference to the writings of people like St Teresa of Avila and St John of The Cross, I went to their original writings for myself and soon bought second-hand copies of their works too. I read all the English mystics particularly liking Walter Hilton's *Ladder of Perfection* [*Scale of Perfection*].

I am nothing, I have nothing, there is nothing I seek or desire save to love Jesus with all my heart, with all my soul and with all my mind and all my strength and to be with him forever at Jerusalem.[6]

I also read *The Cloud of Unknowing*, and the writings of Julian of Norwich and Richard Rolle. Richard Rolle was to interest me again later on when I was seeking to find out more about the Fire of Love. In those early days I was hoping to learn to pray and to seek encouragement and affirmation, and to learn more about prayer from the great writers of the past, in the hope that I could again find the God I had already encountered. As I was living my life of prayer mainly on my own, I particularly needed to have the support that came from reading the lives and accounts of other people and their teaching and experience. Indeed I did find a lot of affirmation through the reading I was able to do, but generally I found very few other people who had been put in a position of having to reconcile so many responsibilities, that were obviously a God-given duty, with a deep call to prayer. In every sense it has been a very hidden life, camouflaged by its very ordinariness. I very often did have times of doubt in my own calling though, as it did not seem to be one that was to be expected to come to a young person such as I was.

> Smite upon the dark Cloud of Unknowing with a dart of longing love. Whenever your mind is occupied with anything physical, however praiseworthy, you can be said to be 'beneath' yourself and 'outside' your soul.[7]

The power of that inner call was almost irresistible and yet time and space were rarely available. The deep, still place that I had discovered in the depth of my mind, my heart, were there, like a mountain lake hidden away, yet always there. In time of prayer I had only to focus my mind on it with quiet attention, looking beyond the thoughts and feelings that were on the surface, rather as one would look over the garden wall into the uncultivated and unoccupied land that was beyond the boundary.

As I said, that deep, still place was always associated, for me, with the presence of Jesus. One day, after getting so completely lost in that silence and stillness, I felt an inner fulfilment that I had never known in my life before in any way, and I knew that I had at last discovered the purpose of my creation. 'This is what I was created for,' I said to myself. I realized that until then I had never really known what my real calling was, and the knowledge of at last having found it was deeply nourishing in a way that I had never been nourished before. That conviction and insight gave me strength to persevere.

> Amma Syncletica said, There are many who live in the mountains and behave as if they were in the town, and they are wasting their time. It is possible to be a solitary in one's mind while living in a crowd, and it is possible for one who is a solitary to live in the crowd of his own thoughts.[8]

> Contemplation is not the pleasant reaction to a celestial sunset, nor is it the perpetual twitter of heavenly birdsong. It is not even an emotion. It is the awareness of God, known and loved at the core of one's being.[9]

It is important to recognize the truth of those sentiments; I have met many people who, having had some sort of spiritual experience and insight, have seemed to me to become rather ungrounded. It is a temptation to think that because we have had some spiritual experiences we are well on the way. There is always a risk of spiritual inflation and spiritual pride and it is possible to become even more self-centred but in an elitist and selective way, a way that is therefore even more dangerous. If we have a good grounding in the teaching of the early Church Fathers and the great tradition of the past history of the Church this risk may be avoided. Spiritual experiences are gifts to help us on our way but are certainly not ends in themselves; see St Teresa of Avila and Ruth Burrows' *Guidelines for Mystical Prayer*. It is only if we can persevere through darkness and continue being faithful to our outward duties, that we may know that our faith is real and that we are drawing near to God. Jan van Ruusbroek also speaks of a 'person's desiring to be something or thinking that he is something already, or to his ascribing something to himself or thinking that he has earned the feeling of consolation and is worthy of it.'[10] It is a great danger to think or feel something along those lines, and to think otherwise is a falsehood. This is not to say that we are not made in the image of God and are not loved by him, but we are much more than we think we are, not just existing at the level of personality and 'self-centredness'. This has yet to be discovered.

Sometimes a beautiful sunset may indeed remind us of 'the glory of God'.[11] For example, to be aware of the presence of God in the beauties of nature and creation can be an invitation to seek him at a deeper level. To see people shining with his love reveals something that is true and beautiful; we are all indeed made in the image of God. However, these glimpses are by no means essential nor are they a sure sign of contemplative prayer, though they may sometimes be given to us as an encouragement on our way, in fact Fr Thomas Keating says that some people need such experiences simply because they are not strong enough to grow without them.

Notes
1. Jn 15:16.
2. Lk. 17:21 (NIV).
3. Augustine of Hippo from Sermons 261, 2.
4. Mt. 7:7; Lk. 11:9.
5. Origen, *On Prayer*, 12 (PG 11, 452).
6. Walter Hilton, *Scale of Perfection*.
7. *The Cloud of Unknowing*, p. 67.
8. *The Sayings of the Desert Fathers*, p. 196.
9. Clifton Wolters, Introduction to *The Cloud of Unknowing*, p. 36.
10. *The Spiritual Espousals, Classics of Western Spirituality* Series, p. 83.
11. Ps. 19.

Chapter Two

The Cloister Within

Seek no more abroad, say I,
House and Home, but turn thine eye
Inward, and observe thy breast;
There alone dwells solid Rest ...
And keep House in peace, tho' all
Th' Universe's fabric fall.[1]

Right from the beginning the very act of trying to follow the call itself will make us aware of anything that comes between ourselves and that deep, still, inner place – in that place where words fall away and there is only the need to listen and receive. It is the beginning of the development of the cloister within. I have found over the years that the call to interior prayer creates its own discipline. It demands that we accept our vocation in faith and obedience just as we are, wherever we are, whatever the outward circumstances. The important thing is to learn to listen to the Spirit's guidance and, certainly in the early years, it is good to have someone we can trust and whom we respect, to give support and guidance, though there may come a time later on when we have to dare to take a more risky and a more solitary path.

Spiritual Loneliness

There are roads suitable for all vocations and all are going the same way and to the same end. There is the highway up the valley floor with no very great ascents but a steady climb winding up into the mountains, and in bands and with the mutual support of numbers the pilgrims stream up the road – we thank God for them. On the hillsides in the tracks through the uplands more direct paths are traversed by little groups encouraging each other in fervour and pointing the way to those below – we thank God for them.

But higher on the mountains there are more direct ways, often on the very edge of precipices amid winds and mist, and on these ways go folk who by the very necessity of their way go solitary and yet are encouraged by the knowledge of each other. We thank God for them as they are called to pioneer the way and to encourage those who follow to be amongst them because of our knowledge that it is only His Grace that can keep us steadfast and progressing amid the heights and storms. It is His Way and His calling and that is sufficient for us.

The straight way crosses many watersheds, mountaintops on which the clear air may stimulate and the light and shade increase vision, but there are many valleys, deep and dark, that stretch between the heights and they must be steadfastly gone through. On the hilltops we may see and rejoice with our companions who go the same way, but in the darkness of the valleys we may seem to be alone as if no other was on the way and as if we had left the height for ever, and yet the very next slope is before us and it would be lack of humility not to face the ascent. It is all the Lord's work and as the prophet wrote – there shall be a way and even fools shall not err therein.

There are two lonelinesses, one that comes from the status of vocation, that if one is called to the heights one stands outside the comprehension and pattern, of the lower roads, yet having to understand them without displaying a pride that would hinder our own vocation. It is only as we know that as the Bride we have sought and been found and in the humility of our abnegation we realise the truth – 'His desire is towards me', that we can travel the uplands.

The other loneliness is of the Way itself, and our confidence is that it is His Way, the being in His work of reconciliation in making satisfaction, and in that confidence we stand and go on standing in God, His Love and His Peace.

The guile of the enemy would seek to attack on the fundamental virtue of humility, and our answer is surely that it is not our choice, but the Lord's and the doing is his work. I come back to St Paul's 'who is sufficient ...' and that is why I mention the parable of the descents into the valleys in which the darkness envelops and through which, if we were not in Christ, we could not continue. It is another way of expressing the light and darkness of which St Teresa speaks, in the Sixth Mansion, of the Betrothal and which is marked in some of the early Easterns as the confusing assaults of the demon on those in the third way of humility.[2]

The call to prayer does itself cause us, though often unknowingly, to live by the monastic principles. Jesus said, 'if you would be perfect, come, leave all that you have to the poor, and follow me'. These are the foundation of the vows of Obedience, Poverty and Chastity. Obedience is to follow the call without question, Poverty is letting go of anything that comes between us and the life of prayer, and Chastity is not only chastity within our state of life but also aiming towards simplicity and the virtue of purity of heart. As we try to follow the attraction, to pray we will immediately become aware of anything that prevents us from following those principles.

Because of my connection with the first religious community that I had encountered, I had learned about the value and meaning of the Divine Office, the 'work of the church'. It was good to know that by sharing in that 'work' we were sharing in the work of the whole Church. Wherever and whenever the Office was being said, we could participate in it and help in the work of prayer for the world and join in the prayer of the Angels and Archangels too. I was not able to say much of the Office in those early days but in time I did begin to get to know and love the psalms, particularly Psalm 119 which was in those days the basis of the daily Offices. Certain verses of that psalm were soon learnt by heart and came to mind frequently during the day. To keep a balance between personal prayer and the liturgy and bible study is essential for a holistic Christian life and I was fortunate in having been grounded in that way though I didn't realize it at the time.

When shall my ways be made so direct that I may keep them forever.[3] Make me to go in the path of your commandments for that is my desire.[4]

Lord, you have searched me out and known me, you know my sitting down and my rising up; you discern my thoughts from afar ... indeed there is not a word on my lips but you, O Lord, know it altogether. Surely the darkness will cover me and the night around me come to light – darkness is not dark to you; the night is as bright as the day, darkness and light to you are both alike.[5]

These words always have great meaning for me. The emphasis on light through darkness and darkness through light always seems very significant. These and many other verses from the psalms became known by heart and would return to mind in different situations.

My family grew up, and I continued trying to learn to pray and to do spiritual reading (*lectio divina*), and to study and to live my vocation in family life. I did often have times of doubt as to whether God had made a mistake in giving me those two vocations at once, but the call had been, and still was, very strong and I knew that there was no other way for me, the calling couldn't be denied.

Be careful at first not to give yourself, nor your whole affections, nor your intimate friendship to anyone unless you have already received the gift and spirit of discretion by which you may know whom to avoid and whom to approach.[6] Until you achieve this be straightforward and friendly while remaining a little aloof from everyone – always excepting the duty of Christian kindness.

These teachings from Walter Hilton are very important and may need to be returned to again and again. It is easy to make the mistake of thinking that everyone will understand our way and we may look in vain for like-minded people with whom to share. It is a lonely pathway and I knew it had to be, we do have to be discreet when talking to other people about our own beliefs and experiences. That loneliness is part of the vocation and accompanies the inner solitude that goes with it.

When our children were in their teens, my husband became very much involved in civic life and served on the Urban District Council for many years. I was able to support him in all that that involved – we had to attend many civic functions: dinners and other social events. I remember, at one of the official dinner dances, a lady saying to me that it wasn't possible to live a contemplative life in the world. I didn't answer her. What was there that I could say?

> We must therefore pray in the heights, depth, length, and breadth of our spirits. Not in many words but in little words of one syllable.[7]

These were indeed my own sentiments by which I tried to live. By that time I was at a fairly even stage in my life and had learned to adjust and balance between outer duties and inner calling, and was ready when the occasions of further growth came my way.

Notes

1. Francis Turner Palgrave, 'Home', in *Treasury of Sacred Song*, London, 1890.
2. Quoted by Fr Gilbert Shaw, late Warden of the Sisters of the Love of God.
3. Ps. 119:5.
4. Ps. 119:35.
5. Ps. 139.
6. Walter Hilton, *Eight Chapters on Perfection*, p. 5.
7. *The Cloud of Unknowing*, p. 67.

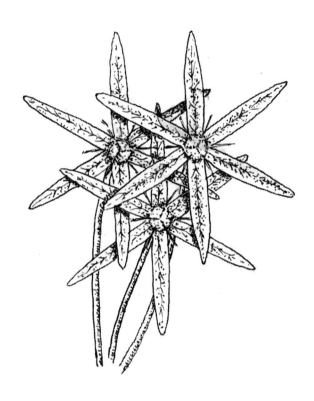

Chapter Three

Further Steps on the Way

In my late thirties I had the opportunity to train to teach. I had seen an advert in the local paper asking for mature people to train and I saw the chance to make up for the fact that, having grown up in wartime, I had had a rather sporadic education. Fortunately, most of the schools I went to were what could be called 'good schools' and they taught us to speak properly and emphasized the importance of good manners. Those things had given me some basis for the outer side of my life and, to some extent, helped my to get by and covered over my lack of book learning. I have long since come to see that courtesy and respect for other people are foundational to the Christian life. Once we come to see that God is present in the depths of every human being and in everything created, we know that we relate to and serve him with love and compassion in other people.

As I was growing up, my lack of education had always been a source of self-consciousness and that gave me a sense of not being like most other people. Later I realized that mere book learning and academic qualification were not enough to help a person on the way to the wholeness that I was seeking, though my own aspirations were probably still rather instinctive and intuitive at that stage. In fact, over the years I met a number of people who, whilst being expert in their own field of learning, were nevertheless often lacking in the ability to relate to others with compassion and understanding.

However, when the opportunity came to make up for what had seemed a great deprivation, I was delighted to be able to take the chance. I had to take some GCE O-level courses before I could be admitted to the college course and the fact that I did so well in those was very stimulating and affirming to me. My husband and his family were very supportive and I will always be grateful to them for that. The opportunity to take a three-year course at a College of Education (Post Graduate Teaching Certificate) was a great blessing to me in many ways. I can honestly say that I enjoyed almost every minute of it and worked very hard, attaining very pleasing results at the end. Later on, when it dawned on me how great was the deprivation I had suffered, I felt very angry and that had to be faced and dealt with. But later still, I realized that that very deprivation had in fact caused me to rely much more on my own inner resources, and so made me stronger than I otherwise might have been. It is rather like a tree that had been planted without much support, but the fact that it had to bend to and fro in the winds had made it much stronger than if it had been tied to stakes.

All things work together for the good of them that love God.

My Spiritual Director said that the fact that I enjoyed the college course so much was a sign that I was meant to do it. I was glad to have his affirmation as I might have wondered if I was walking away from my call to be a contemplative, but the inner call was much deeper than outward things and would not be lost as long as there was faith. I think that by that time I had gone beyond the point of no return; my commitment to prayer as a foundation of my life was already sealed.

As well as the Theory and Practice of Education, I studied Art and Craft as two separate main subjects and discovered creativities that I never knew I had. It was a time of great blossoming and gaining in outer confidence.

At the end of the course I was offered a teaching post in a recognized independent prep school for boys where I was in charge of the Art and Craft department. Life seemed settled and good. All during the years at college, and when I started teaching, I continued to keep a regular pattern of prayer and recollection. This consisted of 'smiting upon the Cloud of

Unknowing with a dart of longing love'[1] both in set times of prayer, when I had the opportunity and, even more importantly, by making frequent acts of recollection during the daily round. I had the nourishment of attending daily Mass whenever possible and of course saying part of the daily Office and spiritual reading, and an occasional retreat. I never lost my belief in the conviction of Christ's presence within me in an immediate way as I lived my daily routine of running the home and attending college or school. It was a time of growth and consolidation in prayer with continual adjustment and readjustment to living a life of prayer in the world. A time for maturing, for gaining confidence in my vocation and for strengthening and, unknowingly, building a foundation for the next stage. I expect it was what St John of the Cross would call the stage of proficients or a plateau stage.

> We must therefore pray in the heights, depth, length, and breadth of our spirits. Not in many words but in little words of one syllable.[2]

This quotation continues to be perfect advice for those seeking to live a contemplative life, hidden and yet in the world. It again stresses the need for balance in all parts of our selves and reminds us that our aim in life is not to become 'something' in our own right and from our own centre, but to allow ourselves to be transfigured into a likeness of Christ and to be a channel of his healing and redemptive love for the world.

During those years that I was teaching I had kept up my four-weekly visits to Fr Slade and on one occasion I told him that I had an attraction to a kind of emptying prayer, it seemed like an inarticulate desire to pour myself out and have nothing in my mind that was of my own making. He seemed to be aware of something in what I said and he remarked that 'something wonderful' would happen to me quite soon, and it did.

Notes

1. *The Cloud of Unknowing*, 67.
2. Ibid.

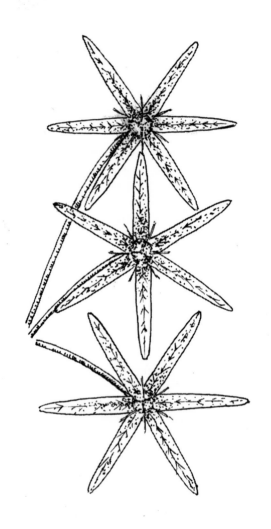

Chapter Four

Finding the Door, 1973

After the Christmas school holidays came a quieter time in the stillness and emptiness that follow after the celebrations are over; there was the darkness and quiet peace and space of winter. I had time for a peaceful routine again. My children were past their teens by this time and were living their independent lives; and my husband was at work during the daytime. I just carried out the routine of running the home and had a time for prayer during the afternoons. I continued to be aware of the attraction to 'emptying' prayer, by which I mean a desire to sweep everything out of my mind, as if I was taking a broom and sweeping everything over the edge of a cliff, to have nothing left within. In the stillness of that prayer I became aware of an open door, which appeared in the darkness of my own mind. I hadn't noticed it before but there it was, and it seemed quite natural just to enter in. After several visits through the door – this period lasted for about three weeks – I began to see things in a new and very different way.

When I went down into the garden, flowers and plants had taken on a new radiance and integrity of their own, they seemed to be pregnant with life and wanting to communicate with me. Even stones by the roadside, when I walked up to do the shopping, seemed to have their own meaning and appeared to want to communicate; it was as if they too were pregnant with radiating life.

I became aware of a great sense of unity, empathy and compassion for, and with, other people. I could see and comprehend very vividly that all people are equal in God's eyes. No one person is more valuable than another to him. There was also a vivid awareness that, by being in that space myself, I was somehow helping other people on their way too; it was clear to me, that it wasn't just for myself that I was following that call. It was some years before I came to see that that is a true sign of an authentic spirituality and is what is meant by helping in the work of redemption and reconciliation, even though one might not always, or indeed very often, be consciously aware of it. I now believe, since I had that convincing experience of the unity of all people in God, that inasmuch as we try to follow the vocation to pray we are living a life of intercession for the world, even though not always expressed in words to any great extent. Inasmuch as we try to live in the centre ourselves, we take other people with us.

Naturally there were people and causes to be prayed for individually but the whole of my life now could be seen to be one single, simple act of prayer and intercession because it was an attempt to follow a call that was both inner and outer; and to follow it by obedience that was also both inner and outer thus was helping in the work of redemption. I also realized that by trying to accept the difficulties or even sufferings that come in everyday life with as much patience as possible was in itself an act of intercession for other people, even for people I did not know or had never met. Those difficulties, though often quite insignificant in themselves, seemed to me to be a small type of the cross, and to accept them as peacefully as possible is the way to life and growth.

The pathway to the open door that had become apparent to me was approached by an outpouring of myself, a self-surrender that came from the very depths, from a level much deeper than verbal thought. It could only be approached after having been given some sense of an invitation and knowledge of it, otherwise it would have been a product of my own efforts and it certainly wasn't that. On the contrary it could only be found when following a strong, almost passionate desire to have nothing in my mind that was of my own making. Although I wasn't able to put it into words at that time, I was in fact learning to grow into the way of *apatheia*, the *via negativa*. I was beginning to learn from my own experience that God is beyond and above all creation and that any created thing, however beautiful or good, would never be enough for me.

I was vividly aware how transitory all previously familiar spiritual concepts were and I had an inarticulate yet urgent hunger to be without anything that was in any way tangible. There was a sense of groping and striving to pour myself out in response to an invitation to have nothing that was of my own making. As the invitation became more vivid I learnt how to respond and then came the new way of seeing things – a new standard of values. It was like living on a different level, a different stratum almost. Humility was seen as a golden secret and is the greatest and most worthy of all gifts – it is not merely a virtue along with other virtues, it really is of the Truth. The way we live in the world, the usual values and criteria are seen to be all shot through with a big mistake – they were/are all self-centred appertaining to our own seeming good; achievements, success, possessions, status and attainment. Such efforts, when they get out of proportion, but only when they get out of proportion – because of course the desire to work for good in the world or to use the creativity we have been given is a vocation in itself – are the cause of all the trouble and discord and disunity which afflicts the world; a blind error that affects the whole of mankind. I was so convinced of the reality of this that I longed for everyone to know it. I wanted so much to share the good news that I had found. I saw that all of creation, and created things, have an immense value simply because they were created by God; there would always be a sense of reverence and respect for all of creation after that insight. In this new way of being there was a great sense of belonging, being at home in the place where I was always meant to be. I could see that there should be no division between people; all people are of equal value in the sight of God. I could also see that Christ is not to be contained only in the Christian Church. He is too big to be confined by any man-made structure or organisation, too great to be contained by anything that has been created.

I also knew that I myself would always be faithful to the

Church because it was through the Church that I had found God. To have left it or to change in anyway would imply that I was disloyal and ungrateful and was taking matters into my own hands in a self-centred way. The Church was the way through which I was meant to grow, though I knew it was not the only way to come to know that God is Love. The Church does have its shortcomings indeed but to desert it would only be making things worse, it would be denying God's love and providence for me and would be attempting to take my life into my own hands instead of trusting in him and his providence for me.

When that door was open it was possible to live by the standards that it enlightened so clearly. And so the time of insight continued for the remainder of the school holidays and for a short while after I returned to my work as a schoolteacher, about three weeks altogether.

Chapter Five

Descent to Contrition

O Lord, you have promised to make your home with the contrite and humble of heart * so fill our hearts with your grace that we may become a people in whom you are pleased to dwell.[1]

After that time of insight and illumination, I had to learn that there was another side of the page and that God does not always allow us to live on the mountaintops for long. The descent may be brought about by many different circumstances. For me it was because, after the Christmas holidays, I had to return to my obligations as a schoolteacher as well as keeping up with my family life. There was very little time to be quiet and peaceful, and my work and lifestyle were very demanding, mentally, physically and socially. The descent is unlikely to come about because of any intentional wrongdoing. I was certainly not aware of any of that in myself and I feel sure that I would have realized it at once if it had been my own deliberate fault. As I got involved in schoolwork again, together with running the home, I felt, spiritually, as if I was slipping and sliding down a mountainside – unable to get my footing, grasping and clutching, and yet the descent continued. It seemed a terrible thing to have seen the place that I was always meant to be in and yet know that I was unable to get there by my own efforts and endeavours. My outer calling seemed to contradict my inner inclination and capacities. The memory of that other level was still there but was now only a memory not an experience. It was heartbreaking to see old values returning and yet be helpless. The word penitence took on a new and deeper meaning – reconciliation, contrition – and, though I was not aware of it at the time, there was a broadening and deepening of knowledge and wisdom, and a continuation of the sense of helping in the work of redemption on behalf of others.

In the meantime, it was a return to the humble pathway of diligence in the duties of state of life and trust in God. I never really doubted that God's will was revealed both within and also in outer responsibilities, and I knew that the two had to come together, but it was not an easy path to follow. Now, when I look back over the years, it is as if the truths I learnt in those insights were to be relived and re-learnt over and over again. It was as if what I had seen had to change into becoming something of what I actually was. Instead of seeing a view from afar, I had to be really living in the landscape.

> When the grace of devotion is withdrawn and you undergo temptations and great troubles you must pray no less than when you have grace without temptation. And whatever troubles and temptations you may meet, never stop praying, either as you carry on your business in the world, with other people, or alone.[2]

About six weeks after my returning to school life, there was a potentially fatal illness to be faced which involved surgery and, after a recurrence of it a year later, a time of seeming total inability to pray for over four years. It was a time of darkness that perhaps might be equated with the night of the senses that St John of the Cross describes. I expect the loss of ability to pray was partially influenced by physical debility and the sense of having lost my way spiritually, or at least having lost the ability to get back to where I had been. Of course, as I was to understand later, it was not at all a matter of going back to where I had been but waiting until the time came to move on.

The old patterns of prayer and the intention of recollection, continued. I took at least twenty minutes every evening, seeking to focus on the place within myself where God had been found before. But the door was not only shut, it was totally invisible. Yet there was still the memory, so clear and yet so unattainable. The hidden value of this time did not become clear for decades but in fact I later came to see that it had been invaluable for building a foundation for the future. The insights experienced and the lessons learned during that time were to be a source of the integrated foundation of my life, to be lived and returned to over the next thirty years, though I was prompted to return by intuition, faith and memory rather than by conscious thought, experience and effort.

The basic conviction that I had of the unity of the whole of humanity and the truth and value of humility remained constant, although they were often covered over by my response of fear or anxiety in the many circumstances and events that came to me on my way. Nevertheless the truth was always there and helped me through. The way to keep the connection was to persevere in contemplative prayer as well as I could.

> Meister Eckhart: 'if you cannot find God, look for him where you last met him'.

> He prays unceasingly who combines prayer with necessary duties and duties with prayer. Only in this way can we find it practicable to fulfill the commandment to pray always. It consists in regarding the whole of Christian existence as a single great prayer. What we are accustomed to call prayer is only part of it.[3]

I was indeed trying to find God where I had last met him, remembering the way I had learnt and offering myself as best as I was able, and in time things did change again and new things were to be learnt. I had gone on as best I could, still keeping up the routine of giving time to quiet prayer every day and hoping that things would change again. I often used to seek someone to talk to about it all but seldom, if ever, found anyone. My first spiritual director had moved further away and I couldn't get to see him as often. When I did, he wasn't very sympathetic, saying why shouldn't I have times of darkness, he had had them too. On one occasion he quoted from the legend of Psyche: 'I heard a voice behind me saying "this is the way, walk ye in it"', this was indicating that the truth was there waiting to be discovered from within myself. Growth was taking place in the darkness, just as bulbs grow beneath the soil in winter, unknown and unseen until the right time comes for them to emerge and for the blossoms to appear.

> If we become aware that we have strayed from God, then we should leave all things and go quickly to the Temple, which means to say that we should gather all our faculties in our inner Temple in our deep ground. When we have fully withdrawn there, then we shall without doubt find God and know Him again.[4]

> A man was looking for the key to his house; he searched in the long grass outside the door. Some friends came to help him, spending hours looking for the key. After a while they said 'are you sure that you lost the key out here?' 'Oh no,' he said,' I lost it inside the house but there is more light out here.'[5]

We are often inclined to seek answers to our problems and searchings outside ourselves and in outer solutions, we turn to the 'expert' for advice or run away to 'somewhere else', when all the time the answer may be within our own deepest being. All will be revealed at the right time and when we are ready to hear it.

Notes
1. Collect for Week Six.
2. Walter Hilton, *Eight Chapters of Perfection*, pp. 2–3.
3. Origen, *On Prayer*.
4. Johannes Tauler.
5. Thomas Keating, OCSO, *The Human Condition – Contemplation and Transformation*, pp 8–9.

Chapter Six

Moving On

By this time I had also moved on in outer ways. After my illness, the religious community that I had been connected with were very concerned about my health. They offered me the use of a studio room for a small rental in which I could start my own pottery business. Ceramics was one of the subjects in which I had been well taught whilst at college and I felt confident that I could now work on my own. The Sisters installed water and a sink in the studio and gave me a large table to work on, so I had the rudiments of all I needed to begin to set up the pottery. We had been left a bit of money at that time and so I was able to buy a kiln and a potter's wheel and to assemble a complete pottery workshop. At first I continued school teaching, just working in the pottery in spare time but as the business began to grow, I retired from teaching and ran the pottery as a part-time business; my husband used to help me with some of the heavy work in the evenings and at weekends. I felt that creative and manual work was as near as I could get to a contemplative way of life, so at that time it came very near to being a perfect lifestyle for me.

I had carried the words that described that time of insight that came with 'finding the door' round in my head for four years, continually returning to dwell on all that it had taught me, until one busy Sunday morning when my husband and I were getting ready to take some of my pottery to a Craft Fair. I couldn't keep it in any longer; I just sat down on the settee with an old exercise book and wrote it straight off as fresh as if it had only come yesterday. The insights gained during that time have been something to return to and meditate on for the rest of my life.

> Yet the abstinence in which he [the contemplative] lives should not be excessive, nor on the other hand should he display too much extravagance ... The true lover of Christ, one who is taught by him, does not worry overmuch whether there is too much or too little ... I, myself have eaten and drunk things that are considered delicacies; not because I love such dainties, but in order to sustain my being in the service of God, and in the joy of Christ, for his sake I conformed quite properly with whom I was living lest I should invent a sanctity where none existed.[1]

Once the call has been recognized and accepted, the Holy Spirit will make it clear to us whether or not we should practise fasting or other self-disciplines. The aim of our life is union with God not self-perfection, and we must always try to be aware of what helps in keeping balanced in body, mind and spirit.

A very providential event occurred one day when I was working in the pottery. The outer door was open and a man wearing a clerical collar came in and said, 'What is going on here?' If he had been in lay clothing I would have said, 'I am making ceramic birds of prey to sell at the Craft Fairs', but as he was a priest, I replied, 'I am trying to live a life of prayer in the world'.

He replied, 'Oh, you ought to go to Fairacres, the home of The Sisters of the Love of God in Oxford'. I kept in touch with him and reminded him of his suggestion until he got me an introduction. The first time I went to that convent, I knew that I belonged there and I asked to become an Oblate on my first visit. There were so many connections with the Carmelite saints that I had been reading for many years, that I felt immediately at home. There was also a great emphasis on silence and solitude, which was certainly not a problem for me.

Over the years one of the greatest privileges we had in being there was the wonderful library, to which I had access. I had already been saying part of the daily Office, and in that monastic community the Office was a priority, and I was glad to continue to get to know the Psalms. I was still in that time of four years of darkness and seeming inability to pray when I went there but refrained from saying anything about it at the time. I just went on trying to live by the principles of the Rule of the community because I felt that that was where I wanted to be and where I felt at home. I had immediately recognized that reconciliation and helping in the work of redemption was a prime factor in their life and, as that had a great meaning for me too, it was not surprising that I felt at one with them as soon as I arrived. It is interesting, on looking back, that I felt myself to be so at home there even though personal prayer was still so barren for me at that time.

As an Oblate of that community I had the privilege of meeting and hearing some very knowledgeable theologians and writers, one of whom, Fr Donald Allchin, was to be particularly supportive of me, and it was through him that I had the opportunity to attend some courses on theology in the University. I particularly appreciated the course on Greek Mystical Theology by Bishop Kallistos Ware and, amongst others, the one on St Teresa of Avila given by Rowan Williams and a course by Simon Tugwell, who wrote *Ways of Imperfection*.

As I said at the beginning, I have always felt that the early Fathers and Mothers of the Church have a gold mine to offer us today and that the Orthodox writers[2] seem to offer a more holistic approach to life and prayer than many Western theologians – theirs was a teaching that seems to involve more of the whole person, body, mind and spirit, whereas some Western writers sometimes seem to me to be rather more cerebral and academic. I am of course, not a theologian by any means, though I was glad to read that the Orthodox have a saying that 'a Theologian is a person who prays and a person who prays is a Theologian'. I have found much encouragement and affirmation from their writings.

Notes

1. Richard Rolle, *The Fire of Love*.
2. Some sources would be: George Maloney, SJ, a modern writer and priest who was ordained according to the Byzantine rite; Symeon The New Theologian (b. 947); Gregory Palamas; Gregory of Nyssa (b. 350), especially *The Life of Moses* and *From Glory to Glory*, texts from Gregory's mystical writings; Vladimir Lossky, author of *The Mystical Theology of the Eastern Church*; Olivier Clément, *The Roots of Christian Mysticism*.

Part Two

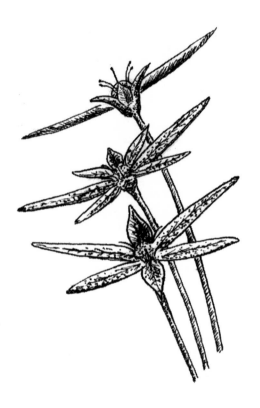

Chapter Seven

Energies

One evening when I was in that seemingly endless time of four years of darkness and inability to pray that followed my illness, I had an experience of a coming of energies. I had continued to keep up my routine of offering myself in quiet but ostensibly unheard and unnoticed prayer. On that particular evening as I was walking upstairs for my usual prayer time, it suddenly came to me that I knew what attitude of mind God wanted me to take in prayer. It is impossible to describe what I mean by that, but the sense of knowing what to do was very clear. When I knelt to pray and put my mind in that certain attitude, the golden energies came. It was quite unexpected and totally surprising. I didn't know what to make of it, as I had not heard of such a thing before. I knew it was a good feeling and it attracted me to pray more in such a way so as to make room for it.

The energies had first come to me like a gentle shower of golden rain, or perhaps it could be said, like a mixture of champagne and sunshine, a golden sparkling warmth. They came suddenly after those years of darkness and difficulty in prayer that had followed the time of ill health; those years which had seemed very long because there was no way of knowing if or when they would ever end.

> When spiritual joy comes to the body from the mind, it suffers no diminution by this communion with the body, but rather transfigures the body, spiritualizing it. For then, rejecting all evil desires of the flesh, it no longer weighs down the soul but rises up with it, the whole man becoming spirit, as it is written: 'He who is born of the Spirit is spirit' John 3:6, 8.[1]

I was again fortunate in having some good advice, support and confirmation from someone in the convent, the retired Reverend Mother (Mother Mary Clare, SLG), who recognized what was happening, but it was not at all easy for me to be peaceful about it at first because it was so unknown and very unexpected. I did have one or two good dreams which indicated that it was all good and of God. After a time I got adjusted to living with this type of prayer and it has continued over the years but during that early time there were, for me, one or two major crises.

The first was when I had to deal with some very trying circumstances that arose due to a difficult family situation, which affected me very deeply in an emotional sense. I went into retreat and my director, Mother Mary Clare, SLG at that time, saw it as a situation for spiritual growth as well as emotional pain. I was told to try to be open to the Holy Spirit. I went to my room and tried to do just that, and then energy came again with much greater power than ever before. It suddenly seemed that my heart was alight and my rib cage was lined with fire – the energy came with great power in my hands and feet and around my head. I asked to see her again and she told me that this might be a permanent feature of my life in the future. I certainly felt that I wanted to make myself available if that was to be the case. It had all come as a great surprise again, and time was needed for readjustment and integration of this new way of praying. That period again was not without some doubts but the energy seemed irresistible and to come from another level of my being. I often felt that I did not understand and in fact as I continued to learn over the years, it was not something that was related to understanding but only to faith and trust.

I continued on this pathway of prayer, living my home and family life, trying to live by the Oblate rule, which included reciting part of the daily Office either in church or in my home, and keeping up with *lectio divina*, for the next twenty years. Those years were of an ordinary family life with its usual ups and downs. After seven or eight years in the studio, I had to give up the pottery business because the Sisters needed the room back again. I then began to train as a counselor with a local group and to do some counselling work in the parish. The theme of balance continued to be very important to me.

In 1995 I went to a retreat where I encountered Contemplative Outreach UK, which had been founded by Thomas Keating, OCSO.[2] I found Fr Thomas' books very helpful. In *Open Mind*, *Open Heart*, the chapter on the Night of the Spirit,[3] Fr Thomas describes 'an immense and unnameable energy that is welling up inside'. Of this immense energy he says, 'No one can describe the experience of pure faith. We only know that this immense energy may be experienced by some as impersonal, though it certainly treats us in a personal way'.[4] This is certainly what I was experiencing and I was very grateful to be able to correspond with him about it later on. Because I still had some questions and uncertainties about the energies I was experiencing, and knowing the essential need to keep balanced, I wrote to Fr Thomas explaining what I had experienced with energies. I still had some doubts as to whether I was going the right way in trying to adapt and adjust to this new way of prayer and the advice and confirmation he gave me in his letters were invaluable to me.

Fr Thomas said that whatever I did, I must accept the energies, not try to suppress them or to encourage them, just call on the Holy Spirit to guide me. One thing he said, which was very hard to accept, since that was what I had been doing for decades, was that it was better not to do much 'centering prayer' at this time as, he said, I was already in deep relationship with God because of the energies and it was therefore not good to try to increase that. Another important thing that Fr Thomas said was that living through this type of experience made great demands on physical strength and not to be afraid to take a rest when I felt the need. This was very much a confirmation that I needed, as I know that I had been inclined to push myself too hard sometimes.

The Warden of the Community of which I became an Oblate, Fr Donald Allchin, had previously suggested that I contact Fr William Johnston, SJ[5] and at that time I had been in correspondence with him for many years. He had had similar experiences, which he refers to in one or two of his books. He was again very affirming and I had the privilege of meeting him in London several times when he was travelling to Ireland via Heathrow, and we had some very useful and supportive conversations. He had recommended a very good book by an American Christian lay Minister.[6] In this book, Phil St Romain describes his own experience of the energies. They came to him quite unexpectedly after he had been practising Christian meditation for some years and he describes how he came to adjust and to accept them in his own life. Fr Thomas had also recommended this book though I had my own copy by then. The fact that at last I had found two people (Fr William Johnston, SJ and Fr Thomas Keating, OCSO) who, though they lived on opposite sides of the world, in America and Japan, knew and recognized what was happening, was an enormous help to me and I became more stabilized again. It seems that this phenomenon is occurring in many ordinary people at this time in the history of spirituality and it is good to know that there are people who can give affirmation from a Christian standpoint. By meeting and talking with some of those people and reading their books, I finally came to the conclusion that, although there were many similarities between them, no two people's experiences were identical, therefore I could assume that my own experience would also be unique to me. The way through, so far, has been to have faith and trust in the guidance of the Holy Spirit.

It was interesting to note that Meister Eckhart also refers to 'energy', though perhaps in a slightly different way.

> Eckhart does not speak only of 'melting' but of 'glowing' and of 'boiling'. All this suggests a colossal accumulation of energy, yet all held in total balance and control. This again is the secret to be found throughout the universe, including our own lives. When we act, and pour ourselves out in the world and in relationships with other people, this involves loss of energy, dissipation. But to learn to pour out while remaining inwardly detached, to be at once in movement yet also in repose, is largely what the spiritual life is all about: to the extent that we have learned that we are true persons, true images of God, true sharers in the swirling, glowing, energetic life of the Trinity.[7]

This is what the spiritual life is intended to be: to the extent that we have learned that we are true persons.[8]

Further reading on the subject of fire and energy led me to Dr Lee Sanella[9] and other modern writers; most of them gave me much encouragement and affirmation. I know I would have been very glad to have had more support when I came to this new phase of life in the Spirit myself, yet at the same time I now know that the comprehension of how to live with it had to come from an inner wisdom, from within myself. The people whose books I read were very encouraging and always a resource to be returned to over the years but still could only be general guides and not necessarily infallible for my own condition; again it all came back to faith and trust. At the time of writing, it is over thirty years since the energies came to me and it has taken a long time to understand how to adjust and accept, to live with them in a creative and positive way.

The only thing that got me through was my constant turning to Christ in a simple prayer of faith. I knew that he was at the heart of my being, deeper that I am in myself and he would never leave me; those thoughts enabled me to come through this fiery ordeal and to get stabilized.

There are many dangers on the pathway of prayer. Fr Thomas Keating, writing in *Invitation to Love*, speaks of the subtle dangers that can occur.[10] It can be tempting to think that because we have experienced something of this energy or even of the light, or found ourselves to be in a position of ministering to the needs of others, that we have arrived and that we have all that we need; that we can rely on our own intuition and perceptions, thinking that they are sure to be inspired by God. I have met many people who will confide their spiritual experiences as if they were something special, but when an obvious air of self-satisfaction accompanies this, a sense that they feel that they are special in God's eyes, the experiences are rather questionable. The way to test if the spiritual life is truly and deeply founded in God, will be to note the effect that it has upon our behaviour and attitude; does it bring more self-knowledge, deeper humility, deeper love and respect for other people? At this stage it is valuable to have a soul-friend or someone who will accompany us on our way.

I am still more and more often aware of how hard it is to 'let go' of some situations that arise; often quite small things cause a disturbance, such as a sense of being misunderstood, misjudged or not really heard. Yet in a strange way it is possible to be genuinely thankful for the realization of how I am not always ready to let go. It reassures me that I can still 'fear God' in the best sense of the words, not relying on any gifts that I may feel myself to have or on any progress that I may feel that I have made. Having realized that I am still attached to so many things and situations, makes me aware of how much more room for growth and freedom lie ahead.

As always I continued with spiritual reading and it stood me in good stead, as I continued seeking to learn from reading of others who had similar experiences. I had noticed that the phrase 'fire and light' was frequently used in the writings of the Greek Fathers, particularly St Gregory Palamas who seemed to speak as if to myself, and St Symeon the New Theologian – who is referred to as the Mystic of Fire and Light - and other Orthodox writers. The Orthodox Theologian St Theophan the Recluse says, 'First comes heat and then comes light'.

St John of the Cross, one of the greatest teachers on prayer, wrote, among other books, *The Living Flame of Love*, in which he describes 'the fire that burns but gives no pain'. Other Western writers refer to heat and light; Richard Rolle, whose work I had first read many years before, was an English hermit who wrote a book *The Fire of Love* and he describes a burning fire. A Rhineland mystic, Jan van Ruusbroek, was seen to shine with light as he sat meditating in the woods near Groenendaal. This again confirms my view that the experience of heat and light is and always has been, not uncommon amongst people of deep prayer. I continued with further reading and research. The Bible tells us that the primary basis for 'light' language is the sentence in St John, 'God is light, and in him is no darkness at all' (1 John 1:5). I myself have only seen the energy as light a few times but it did seem to make sense to believe that 'first comes heat and then comes light'. As part of my research, I went to obtain confirmation from an actual person as well as just relying on letters and books. I went to visit the Greek Orthodox priest Bishop Kallistos, whose lectures I had attended earlier, and explained my situation. I took with me my copies of the works of St Gregory Palamas and St Symeon the New Theologian. I was again deeply grateful to receive some very positive reassurance from him.

Another non-Christian book I read, which was recommended to me by a doctor who was also a practising psychotherapist, was *Chasm of Fire*[11] written by a woman in the Sufi tradition; I had the chance to meet her in London later on. In addition I went to a Buddhist Centre and spoke to a nun there, she was affirmative too; but one thing she did say, which sadly turned out to be correct, was 'you will sometimes only have to walk into a room and not even open your mouth and some people will feel threatened by what you have'.

Years later, I came to understand why this is likely to be true and have learnt to cope with it. We are all different and we have to find out how to be who we really are. The important thing is to let others be who they are and treat all with respect even though we may not have much in common as to our approach to life. Even more importantly we must have the courage to be true to our own selves and to follow where we are being led. This can be difficult when we find ourselves in company with others who are on a very different pathway but it is all part of the growing process and the detachment process, and is really very valuable. That Buddhist nun lent me a copy of a work by Gopi Krishna, which I admit I found very disturbing at the time. He had to endure a very hard time for many years. He did come out of it in a stable and selfless state from which he was able to be helpful to many people in many parts of the world.

I have found from my own experience that the energies have been and of course still are, a force for purification and a learning experience that leads towards wholeness and balance. They teach me what I need to let go of and in what way I need to keep mind, body and spirit in tune, in balance. The vindication of it all was that as I got more stabilized again, after those four years in the wilderness, I realized that my life was again on an even keel and was bearing fruit. I knew I had to continue to try to be obedient in complying and cooperating with outer circumstances but that was not done as a duty but as recognition of the fruits of obedience – that is, a total and willing integration into outer circumstances, and the only way to live the Christian life. I then came to know a marvelous freedom and liberty and wholeness that I hadn't known was possible. When I am at peace within myself, the energies too are peaceful and gentle.

As this pathway sometimes seems very strange and not in the least as one would have expected, and certainly not one I would knowingly have chosen, it was sometimes tempting to want to go back and to travel by a more recognizable path. But it is important to acknowledge that it is not possible to go back once this stage has been reached, simply because there is no 'back' to go to. It is as if this part of the journey has been across desert sands and our footprints have been blown away in the wind, there is no trace of the way back, and all that we have been through has effected a radical change in one's outlook and in one's being. After years of trying to offer one's life to God, He has taken one seriously and He now needs to be in charge of what happens. In other words it is, as St John of the Cross would say, the beginning of the passive stage of the journey.

Notes

1. John Meyendorff, *St Gregory Palamas and Orthodox Spirituality*, p. 113.
2. Fr Thomas Keating is a retired Abbot and founder of Contemplative Outreach, and the author of many books on the spiritual life. *Open Mind, Open Heart* and *Invitation to Love* are two that have helped and affirmed me most.
3. *Invitation to Love*, p. 98.
4. Thomas Keating, OCSO.
5. Fr William Johnston, SJ, another well-known writer on the spiritual life.
6. Phil St Romain.
7. Cyprian Smith, OSB, *The Way of Paradox*, p. 35.
8. Ibid.
9. *The Kundalini Experience*.
10. Thomas Keating, OCSO, *Invitation to Love*, p. 96: 'the temptation may arise to identify with the role of gifted teacher, leader, and so on. Success in ministry may lead to identification with an idealized self-image and the person is back in the grip of self-love.'
11. By Irina Tweedie.

Chapter Eight

A Healing Ministry

It was suggested by Mother Mary Clare that these energies were related to a gift of healing, and I was sent off to see the diocesan Bishop. He arranged for me to do a short course of training with a chaplain at the John Radcliffe hospital, and in addition the Bishop asked me to write some essays for him. At about that time I was still doing the five-year training course in pastoral counselling. I had felt that I wanted to learn how to become more available to other people in a practical way if needed, and that training was certainly very valuable, both for myself and for others. After finishing the additional course that the Bishop had prescribed, I went back to see him and he gave me his authority for a Non-stipendiary Ministry for the purposes of Counselling and Healing in the Diocese.

When a new Vicar arrived in our Parish – I think he was rather surprised to find me there with the Bishop's authority – after a while he asked me to help him explore the possibilities of setting up Healing services. He had called a meeting for all those interested in the healing ministry and there was a good deal of interest; quite a lot of people came to the first meeting and so we started having Healing services once a month on a weekday evening.

The services were always centred on the Eucharist, and people were invited to receive the laying on of hands if they wished. There was always a short address after the reading of the Gospel, and I used to take a turn speaking along with the other clergy of the parish. A lot of people would come from quite a wide area around as well as from the parish itself. I think that was one of the best things about the services, they brought a lot of people to church who would not have otherwise come, so as well as the services themselves, there was also a very important outreach.

In addition I was sometimes invited to speak and assist at other parishes in the diocese. After about ten years, the Vicar moved on again, and as my husband's health was beginning to deteriorate, we too moved away from that parish and my authority had to be cancelled due to the fact that I had moved out of the diocese. The Healing services declined and are now no longer held in that parish.

> A whole person reveals the Glory of God
> and the Glory of God is seen in a whole person.[1]

Although I greatly enjoyed being involved in that work and was glad to have met so many lovely people, I cannot honestly say that I ever knew of anyone receiving physical healing. As people grow into wholeness, often psychosomatic symptoms will disappear, healing is not just for the physical cure of the body, it is a movement into wholeness. And there did often seem to be many people who received inner healing for some difficulties in relationships or inner problems of their own. I do know that there was always a very peaceful atmosphere at the services and people very frequently used to remark on it. I am convinced that healing is, or should be, related to wholeness and to the whole person, body, mind and spirit.

I never felt that to be involved with physical healing was my primary vocation. I believed that my main calling was to be a channel of peace[2] and reconciliation for the world and to learn to help in the work of redemption, and this was how I continued trying to live. When the time came for my husband and me to move on, I was easily able to let go of that ministry. Sometimes even now someone will ask me to give the laying on of hands with prayer and I would never refuse, but neither would I go out of my way to be in that position and would always wait to be invited.

Notes

1. From one of the early Fathers of the Church, possibly St Irenaeus.
2. 'Have peace in your heart and thousands round you will be saved', St Seraphim of Sarov.

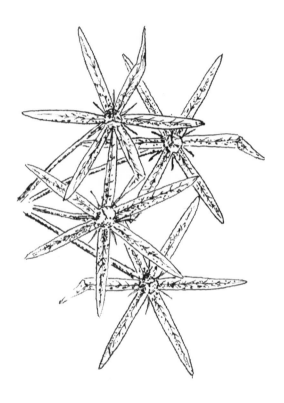

Chapter Nine

Inner Healing –
the Holy Spirit, the Counsellor

Have mercy on me, O Lord, for I am in trouble; my eye is consumed with sorrow and also my throat and my belly ... Make your face to shine upon your servant, and in your loving-kindness same me (Ps. 31:9, 16).

For it has been granted to you, that for the sake of Christ you should not only believe in him, but also suffer for his sake (Phil. 1:29).

On the journey, the 'lure' to be open in contemplative prayer was irresistible; often followed by pain and suffering – emotional fragility and distress, uncertainty and doubt about my vocation, unhelpful attitudes that had been instilled in childhood, all came to the surface in their turn. During the whole time of growth in contemplative prayer, but particularly in the early days, a lot of inner healing took place. This is usual, as prayer deepens and superficial layers of self are revealed and float away and the dark side of the personality has to be accepted and reintegrated. This process is well described in Fr Thomas Keating's books.[1] Perhaps there has been a projection of our own needs into relationships. Unconsciously we still look for deep fulfilment, nurturing and feeding from outside of ourselves, whereas that deepest fulfilment can only be found in union, or at least growing union, with God. Psychotherapy undoubtedly helps and supports some people during this time and when I did my own five years training in counselling, it helped me to a certain extent to understand what was happening, but it is important to remember that psychotherapy is only a tool and not an end in itself.

As understanding dawned, I had begun to realize what was happening and I was able to consent to be healed – to allow the healing to take place. I knew that a time of deep prayer would almost certainly be followed by further emotional pain or instability but once I understood what was going on, I was able to accept and to know this. In those days I couldn't explain this process to anyone else. If I tried to talk about my problems, I could only make them understand the painful part and they would want to heal me in their own way. They wanted to deal with the surface happenings but I knew, in a dark, wordless way, that there was another dimension to it all but couldn't explain it at that time, either to them or even to myself. There was also another kind of pain, a deep spiritual ache which is hard to describe and seemed to come from nowhere and to have no apparent cause or meaning; it continued for many years, and eventually disappeared, only reappearing occasionally after that time.

When I did my training in counselling, I had discovered that I am an 'introverted, intuitive thinking type' of personality.[2] Until then I had imagined that everyone saw things the way that I did and so it was good for me to know that there are other ways of approaching life than that which seemed natural to me. At the same time, I needed to learn and accept that this inborn disposition had to be found and recognized and worked with. To be an introvert in a busy lifestyle is not an easy path but when balanced out over the years it can lead to great fulfilment and richness of life. To find that other people don't always see things the way I did was all a very important learning experience, to let others be and yet to dare to continue also to be myself.

As I said, I was fortunate in having the support of some very high calibre spiritual directors through those years, though some of them did seem a bit harsh at the time. Knowing them was still invaluable to me, as faith can be tested to the utmost and I needed support that I could trust. The past can be redeemed and wholeness, at least at one level, becomes a possibility. I had always felt that the healing was not just for me. As the pain of growth is a small type of the pain of everyone, so by allowing healing to take place it somehow helps others. That realization was always a very important feature in my life. Slowly equanimity was established – balance and integrity could grow and flourish like a healthy plant. Though sometimes when 'the North Wind blows' the scars do still hurt a little.

Notes

1. *Open Mind, Open Heart* and *Invitation to Love*.
2. Jungian typology.

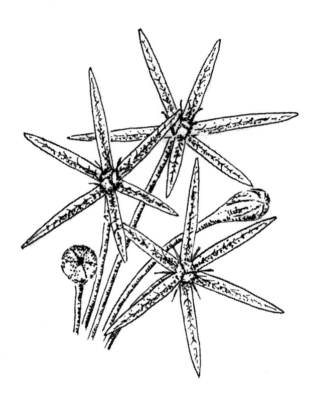

Chapter Ten

The Purpose of the Christian Life is the Acquisition of the Holy Spirit that We may be Transfigured into a Likeness of Christ[1]

The charismatic gifts are for the building up of the body of Christ here on earth. This is a subject concerning which I have seen many people unnecessarily hurt, both by those who think of themselves as being in the Charismatic movement and those outside of it. This seems particularly unfortunate as both groups of people were, in their own way, undoubtedly trying to follow a Christian way of life and of prayer. When a few years ago there was much interest in the Charismatic movement, there was a lot of misunderstanding and therefore criticism, among people who do not have those gifts. In the popular press, the gift of praying in tongues is often associated with a 'happy clappy' attitude but this is only to see it at its most superficial level. Some people, and also groups of people, need this deeper opening up to release their inner potential for service and compassion. I have met many people, men and women, members of the priesthood, in religious communities and among the laity, for whom this gift is a very important part of their own growth and development. I would say that all of those of whom I am thinking also have the gift of a deep life of silent inner prayer and who by no means feel called to use a charismatic gift in company with others but, on the contrary, find it a particularly private gift. St Teresa of Avila, writing in the *Interior Castle*, the Sixth Mansion, speaks of the 'prayer of jubilation' a prayer in which 'Sisters vie with one another as to who can praise God the most'. It is undoubtedly a prayer of praise and thanksgiving but its use, or even reference to it, is what can be the cause of misunderstanding and therefore of painful criticism among those who do not feel called to follow that way. It is of course also a gift that is open to misuse and, as always, the Fruits of the Spirit, Love, Joy, Peace, Patience, and Fortitude are even more valuable than the Gifts of the Spirit. As St Paul says in the First Epistle to the Corinthians,[2] 'though I speak with the tongues of men and of angels and have not charity I am as a sounding brass'. However, we do need to respect others' gifts and callings. That gift can bring the psychological and spiritual breakthrough that some people need and, after receiving that gift myself – it came to me when I was alone and in solitude – I undoubtedly found that I was more able to communicate with other people, to listen to them where they were and on their level. This was because I was able to be less inhibited in myself, having broken through some of the barriers and inhibitions of what had been a rather reserved personality. I was able to be more relaxed and at ease with people in general, so I was able to become more approachable. I also came to be less fearful of who I really was in my own deep self. This development of being able to relate to others in a non-judgemental way is a sure sign of growth in the spiritual life.[3] If the charismatic gifts bring these positive signs then I suggest that we should take care not to be critical or to take a superior attitude towards others' gifts which we may not understand and which therefore do not seem to us to be necessary, but only to seek to be open to those which we ourselves really need and trust God to give them to us. On the contrary, we must always try to respect other people and allow them to wait upon God for their own gifts to come and develop to maturity. We may then be in for some joyful surprises.

Over the years these charismatic gifts may hopefully become so totally integrated into our way of life that all prayer becomes one simple single action.

Prayer is not prayer until it becomes something that you *are* rather than something that you *do*.[4]

Notes
1. St Seraphim of Sarov.
2. Chapter 13.
3. 'The ability to relate quickly to other people is a sure sign of a healing gift', Revd Dr Martin Israel.
4. Fr Gilbert Shaw.

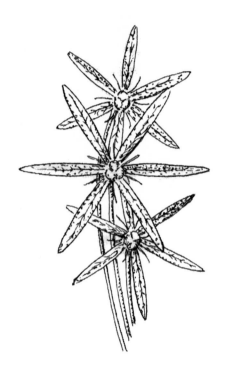

Chapter Eleven

Emptiness

God cannot help but pour Himself into a soul that makes itself empty before him.[1]

The Kingdom of God is within you. Don't look for help from outside, or strain to reason. Now the question arises, whether this birth is to be found in anything which, albeit relating to God, is nevertheless taken in from without, through the senses, in any presentment of God as good, wise or compassionate, or whatever intellect can conceive of divinity ... if this work is to be done God alone can do it.[2]

These sentiments indeed seem to me to belong to the passive way, a development of the contemplative calling, the way where we are led to abandon self and let God do the work. For someone called to the apophatic way, the negative way, these words will come as a great affirmation. God has to be greater than anything he creates or greater than any virtue or gift. There are certain dangers in this way, of course, and this is where it is so valuable to have had spiritual guidance and companionship at least for the earlier years of our journey. It might just be possible that we are following our own inner instincts, which may be influenced by the unhealed experiences and unconscious memories of our past.

Reading *The Way of Paradox* by Fr Cyprian Smith, OSB, was my first encounter with the works of Meister Eckhart and I was very impressed by what he said about detachment. It was something I had been attracted to for a long time in an inarticulate way but that book helped me to put my attraction into words for the first time. I felt that I had discovered that detachment is in fact a form of prayer at its deepest and most profound, and to realize that was like coming upon a priceless and unexpected treasure. Detachment seemed more expansive than prayer itself as it embraced the whole of life in all its activities and experiences, including set times of prayer. It brings one to a very 'immediate' position; a position of responding and surrendering without any intermediary of either thought or image; and so it leads to a marvellous freedom and liberty. In one sense one never goes out of oneself into situations or relationships, and yet by those same situations and relationships one is poured out in an eager and joyful letting go of all one's plans and expectations. There is a kind of obscure knowledge and certainty that this way of seeming loss and seeming poverty will lead to a glorious freedom. If there were not that obscure certainty, such a way would lead to mindless chaos, and so it is a precarious path and perhaps not to be undertaken without invitation.

Before this discovery about the value of detachment, I might have longed for more time and opportunity for more prayer and silence and solitude but this insight into what the essence of deep prayer is, the total surrender of self from a deeper level than any concepts, ideas or images, gives a glimpse of the reality that living and praying can be as one. Then there is an amazed gratitude that this glorious liberty is available, and that it is here and now just waiting to be claimed. At the same time, there was a note of warning which insisted that actual times of prayer should be taken when at all possible and all other obligatory details of one's rule, such as attendance at Mass and Office, and *lectio divina* should be kept faithfully. Though there is no need to be unduly anxious when circumstances make difficulties.

The reason for giving this note of warning was that I had come into this position of insight by way of regular discipline in prayer and spiritual reading, and the teaching of the Christian church and frequenting of the Sacraments. It would have been very unwise and very arrogant to presume that I didn't need to be constantly nourished and sustained by the bread of a regular spiritual discipline.

Of course there will be things and practices to let go of and discernment is necessary. I believed that the Church, in its history as well as in its present, contains the truth and I knew that I would remain faithful come what may. Again it was that intuitive insight that I had had right from the beginning that spoke of the importance of being grounded in both outer and inner circumstances and to keep balanced.

When I read Fr Cyprian's book, I felt that I had come across a gold mine of revelation and was so enthusiastic about Meister Eckhart's teaching that I went up to Ampleforth to meet with Fr Cyprian and to talk about his book and the teaching it held. Although there is much of Eckhart's teaching that I do not understand, to see and to recognize the principles of detachment so clearly illustrated was a great gift and affirmation of my own intuitive feelings on the subject. The talk with Fr Cyprian was also very affirmative for myself and an encouragement to continue to persevere on my own way. It really does seem to me that detachment, letting go and emptiness are a wonderful secret that had been confirmed. The opportunity had always been there in hidden darkness but I had only just had it actually confirmed outwardly. I feel now that I cannot empty myself enough and I wish I could let others know how valuable it is. One of the painful things in this journey of prayer is the longing to share it, but hardly anyone wants to know.

The idea of detachment and emptiness sounds very negative to most people but to some, it will be seen as the way to freedom and joy and, strangely enough, to fullness and also to the ability to communicate with other people just where they are without any of one's own 'agenda' getting in the way of such meetings.

When I first discovered the value and worth of contemplative prayer, all those years ago, I felt I could not get enough of such a good thing. However, after making a few mistakes, I learned by painful experience that it was not good to try to go too fast. It was being proud and self-willed to try to drive myself beyond my capacity, and patient waiting – which has never been one of my best attributes – was the best way forward.

God calls some people to a very austere life, for myself it has always been a mistake to try to drive the body or mind too hard because that way leads to disunity of mind, body and spirit. I am fortunate that I have always enjoyed creative working with my hands and this kind of activity does seem to be very grounding and balancing in a good way.

I continued to become very drawn towards 'emptying prayer'. It began to come alongside the experience of energy and seemed different but also meaningful and almost magnetic in its attraction. I had so often felt that I wanted to pour everything out, it was as if I took a broom and swept everything out of my mind and consciousness, though I could never manage it as much as I felt I wanted to. This call to emptying would begin by a sense of receiving in prayer a little breath like the touch of a feather and I tried to respond by that outpouring action.

After some time I began to see from my own experience how that self-emptying action was having a good effect on my everyday life. I became more aware that I was able to let go of things that had previously caused me some disturbance. Anything that was associated with any kind of difficulty or conflict became easier to abandon and didn't seem to matter so much. This gave me a lot of affirmation, as I knew that if prayer has a good effect on our outer life then it must be sound and wholesome. It seems to me that that is the only way to judge the authenticity of our prayer. I have to say, however, that sometimes the good effects were not always so clearly seen. This outpouring gave me a great sense of liberty and freedom and joy and I could see that it affected my relationships with other people as I was aware that I could make quite deep connections with others simply because I now had not so much of my own agenda to project.

After a time, somehow the prayer of emptiness and the cooperation with the energies began coming together and led me to a greater wholeness. To discover that emptiness is the way to freedom and liberty is a priceless gift. It is not emptiness in a negative way of living for oneself alone but in the way of becoming available for whatever comes along in life in the present moment. It is to do with living in the present without too much regard for past or future. Being ready to share and to give and to care for whoever comes. Not seeking for anything 'to do' for God but just 'being there' for whomever or whatever he sends without any prescribed intentions or methods. I feel that in a good way I am becoming a 'useless servant' and the possibilities seem boundless.[3]

My sense of call to emptiness continued to grow, it was something that had been with me for a long time and it still seemed to be the only way for me. I had learned a little about the way of *apatheia*, the *via negativa*, in my reading of the Greek Fathers. And when I came to read St Gregory of Nyssa[4] who said that 'we go to God from light into darkness' it was like another Eureka moment to me. In a rather inarticulate and inexplicable way it seemed that to have 'nothing' was akin to having 'everything'. If one has 'something' there must be a great deal more that one doesn't have; difficult to explain to anyone who did not have that calling but very real to me. This meant so much to me at that time and I felt that I could see that it was the way that would lead to freedom and growth. We tend to think of ourselves as 'personalities' and to think that our personality is who we are, but the real self is much deeper than the superficial persona and that real self can only be accessed by allowing oneself to be led beyond the persona or personality self. This can only come about during the process of the Dark Night of the spirit.

This is always going to be a very painful experience precisely because it seems to go against what we think of as our own nature and we can only be led through it by the Holy Spirit and in the course of time. I believe that the stages of growth in the spiritual way are rather like biological stages that have to be gone through in unknowingness to allow the development to take place. Like the process of labour and childbirth as I say below, we have to wait for the invitation to walk this dark way and it cannot be pre-empted, but that very willingness to wait is a type of prayer in itself because it speaks of humility and obedience, those keystones of the spiritual life.

Notes
1. Meister Eckhart.
2. Ursula Flemming, *The Man from Whom God Hid Nothing*.
3. See Lk. 17:10.
4. Gregory of Nyssa, *The Life of Moses*.

Part Three

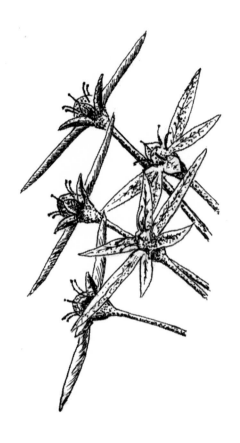

Reflections on the Night

We go to God from Light into Darkness[1]

There is a time when God lives in the soul and a time when the soul lives in God.[2]

Unless a grain of wheat falls to the ground and dies, it remains only a single grain; but if it dies it yields a rich harvest. Anyone who loves his life loses it; Anyone who hates his life in this world will keep it for eternal life.[3]

One day I was standing in my room doing nothing in particular when I suddenly felt as if 'something' had fallen off me. It was as if I had been wearing a warm and protective overcoat and it had suddenly disappeared. My first reaction was to try to get it back on again, but I didn't know what it was that had fallen off or where it had gone. That was the beginning of a long time, at least three and a half years in its greatest intensity, though it continued in a milder way for much longer than that; it was a time of being unable to 'do' anything by an act of my own will-power. I could fulfil all my duties and obligations regarding other people but when I had time on my own it was as if there was some obstruction that prevented me from making up my mind and I would dither about, wanting to 'do' something but not knowing what it was. It was as if there was an invisible barrier in front of me and whichever way I looked I couldn't get past it. Whatever I did do, I knew that that was not what I wanted to do. Whatever I had, I knew that that was not what I wanted to have. I didn't want 'anything' but I did want 'something' and I knew not what it was. It seemed very much like the 'spirit of dizziness' referred to in *The Cloud of Unknowing*.

Later on, I read[4] of something much the same in which the writer described an almost identical incident. She talked about 'the deep deterministic reins of self control' suddenly being taken away and she went on to describe an experience similar to my own. For myself, who had always had the capacity to be very single-minded and determined, it was a great loss and very bewildering. It was as if I had lost my very self, and at a superficial level that is exactly what it was, loss of persona, loss of outer personality self. If it wasn't that I had had confirmation from Bernadette's writing, and two or three moments of very important insights of my own during those few years, I might have thought that it was some sort of depression or even a kind of breakdown. Indeed depression is often one of the symptoms that occur during these times of deep spiritual darkness.

It was not will-power in the sense of wilfulness, that is, wanting to have my own way, that I had lost but the ability to know how to get to where I wanted to be, within myself, and even to know what and where that place was. For so many years I had prayed by putting my attention on that deep still place that was on the other side of thoughts and feelings, rather as you would look over the garden wall at the scenery of the far distant hills; as if there were a deep still lake hidden away up there and that deep still place was always associated with the name and presence of Jesus, the Cosmic Christ. Now, since that falling off experience it was if the lake had disappeared; now I was left high and dry. I had literally lost it and had to find my way through and wait with hope until intuition inspired by the Holy Spirit could take over but that was a slow process and had to happen by degrees. When we have allowed our inner self to be changed and transformed and have come to union with the will of God in our lives, then we will be able to say with St Augustine 'love God and do as you like', in the meantime there is only waiting.

MOMENTS OF ILLUMINATION FROM THE MYSTICAL WRITINGS OF ST JOHN OF THE CROSS

> Sometimes and even quite often, in the midst of aridities and hardship, God communicates to the soul when it least expects it, spiritual sweetness, most pure love, and spiritual knowledge of the most exalted kind, of greater worth and profit than any of which it had previous experience, though at first the soul may not think so, for the spiritual influence communicated is most delicate, and imperceptible by sense (*Dark Night*, Bk 1, ch. 13).

There indeed were some moments of insight that did reassure and prove to me that I was on the right path. On one particular occasion, during a particularly difficult time which had involved house moving and all the stress and strain that comes with that type of experience, as well as being at a loss within my inner self, I was becoming dimly aware that there were further changes in my attitude to people and situations though the sense of it was only very slight at first, just below the surface as it were.

I had had a relative to stay for a few days and when he left on the Saturday morning I went to have a time of rest and relaxation after his visit. I did the Saturday crossword and browsed a few books when I suddenly realized that I was feeling much better than I had for a long time. I was considering why this was when it dawned on me that there had been a process taking place within me, all through that dark time, that had little to do with my own surface efforts and self-chosen activities. I could see that it had begun and I knew it would continue of its own volition.

I saw very clearly that a big change had, and was, taking place, it was as if a fulcrum had moved and was now reoriented in a different direction. Or the process could have been described as being like the movement of a seesaw; one of the ends had moved up when it had been down. It is difficult to explain it more clearly but there was a distinct sense of a change of aim and direction that was taking place from the depths within. I knew that it was not a self-organized change but was a result of being in a state of 'unknowing' for such a long time. It was as if outer ways and situations no longer seemed so very important one way or the other. As I said, the significant thing to note is that this was not a self-chosen movement; there was no way in which it could have been self-chosen because it had been guided from a deeper level than that of usual consciousness. It was an insight that had to come from within myself, which explains why no advice from anyone on the outside could have ever helped me, though I might have continued to seek confirmation.

It dawned on me at that time that whether I got any sense of achievement and attainment from anything I did, or may be called to do, or the way I lived – in good health or not – no longer seemed so very important. I sensed that those things had all been related to the present time and, I realized, my ego self. The importance of all these outer events fell away like a sheath that has been protective but is no longer needed. I could see that my task was to consent to allow this process to continue. This was my vocation, for the time being at least. The real self was now oriented in a different direction. I recognized that this stage was clearly related to the passive way described by St John of the Cross and I could see and feel that it moved towards greater liberty and freedom.

> – ah, the sheer grace! –
> in darkness and concealment
> my house being now all stilled.[5]

As the reality and truth of this dawned on me I knew that I had been shown a great truth which I could not have learned in any other way and its effects are still with me. I was assured of a great confidence in God to take care of my future. The other thing this experience showed me was that I should continue to seek a quiet and peaceful life as much as possible, and to take care of my health. This would help me to keep balanced so as to allow the work to continue. It was as if I was a vehicle in which the process would take place, I have to say that I am sure that this passive attitude is not right for all stages in the life of prayer. There are times when we have to act and then times when it is right to allow God to do the work. This insight gave me great encouragement for a time but darkness again returned. As had happened before, it was now only a memory and not an experience.

Later, there were at least two other occasions which also gave assurance. One was when I had been looking forward very much to some events that I had thought were very important and which ordinarily would have meant a great deal to me. Neither of them materialized but, much to my surprise, I found that I was not deeply disturbed by either disappointment. This, again, came as a great revelation to me, that I had been able to let them go without any conscious effort. Again came the reassurance that 'something' was changing at a deep level that was still largely hidden from me. It reminded me so clearly of the simile of St John of the Cross when he says that the sunshine is only visible when something is in its pathway; then the sunlight can light and illuminate it, otherwise, in pure air, the light is invisible.

As I travelled along the road towards an increasingly simple way of prayer, gradually leaving off all outer aids and just letting myself live *in* the Cloud of Unknowing, rather than *smiting* upon it from the outside as in earlier times, it had become obvious that this increasing simplicity would be bound to lead to loss of self, simply because self was obviously being left behind with the gradual simplifying of prayer. In that sense it was a rather daunting situation to face, and yet it was a road that was irresistible and an inevitable consequence of all that had gone before. There was no alternative but to allow the journey to happen, whatever the cost. With that increasing simplicity of prayer, intention finally moves beyond conscious action and then I was indeed left high and dry.

I found wonderful similes in the writings of St Symeon the New Theologian.[6] No one could put it more clearly than he does and I quote rather fully because I find his writing to be very explicit as to what was happening to me.

2.13: It is like a man standing by the sea. If he is not content just to look, he can go into the waters as deeply as he wants. And if spiritual persons want it, they too can enter into participation with the light of God by means of contemplation, to the extent that they are inspired by desire and knowledge.

You can stand by the flood walls and as long as you are not in the water you can see everything and grasp the whole ocean of water at a glance. But once you start to enter the water and become immersed, then the more you go down into it the more you lose sight of everything outside. It is the same for men who have come to participate in the divine light; the more they progress in divine knowledge, the more they fall into ignorance.

When a man goes up to his knees or even to his waist in the water, he can still see everything outside the water quite clearly, but when he goes down to the bottom and is completely under water he can see nothing of the things outside. He knows but one thing: that he is totally in the depths of the sea. It is exactly the same for men who make progress along the spiritual path and rise to the perfection of knowledge and contemplation.

I quote a later paragraph, 2.16:

When men come close to perfection and yet see it only in part, they are frightened when they realise that it is impossible to grasp or seize what they see. As they penetrate into the light of knowledge, so do they receive an understanding of their own ignorance.

In the Dark Night, the sensual part of the person now rejects any stimulation, as it instinctively and wordlessly knows that it cannot find any satisfaction through the senses. In fact, eating became quite a problem and I could take no interest in any form of pleasure or fictional entertainment. At first this was rather distressing and I couldn't understand why I had this 'dislike' of sense experiences, even the most innocent, but later I was able to give thanks for it and that gave a great sense of freedom again. On the other hand, I always found the beauties of nature, flowers and colour were even more of an inspiration as they reflect the grandeur of God and are a kind of echo of the Glory of God.

The Dark Night is like a gateway into a new state of being. The entrance, which is rather like a foyer, or an anteroom between one larger room and the next, seems strange and incomprehensible simply because it is literally incomprehensible, that is, it is beyond normal ways of understanding. St John of the Cross calls it the night of memory and imagination. Ever since those early insights of the unity of all mankind, I had felt that the mental processes of understanding and knowing are just tools that we have been given to help us live in this world, but I could see that those gifts are not related to our true and deepest selves. As Fr Slade had said, I could sometimes see further than I had got but those truths that had become clear never left me in their essential memory. It was as if, having seen the vision from the mountaintop, I then had to go down into the valley to live it out.

The night of memory and imagination brings with it a seeming inability to use one's usual mental faculties to make decisions; the seeming loss of being able to formulate projects and aims of one's own. As one has grown in prayer over the years there has been much 'letting go' and an increasing simplicity. And this was willingly agreed to, as long as there was a sense of direction, though it seemed inevitable that everything would have to go in the end. When the time does come however, it is not felt to be a good place to be in because it is the very core of 'personality' that is being purged. The natural self continually protests in hidden and diverse ways.

The Dark Night is a way of being that is not related to previous ways, ways of thinking and planning and reasoning; it is a way that seems fathomless and inscrutable and almost frightening. It is in fact a way that will lead to an intuitive state rather than a thinking state but the passage across the foyer has to be travelled first.

In some ways it is similar to the transition from being a child to being an adult. Those years are not always easy; there are times when the teenager wants the security of being a child again and at other times seems to be partly an adult, but before the time is right. Slowly and painfully the transition takes place.

To undertake any specific projects of one's own choice seems impossible; this is because one's objective will-power is now no longer useful, other than for fulfilling simple duties of obligation, and it is, in fact, a hindrance. This is a time for following intuition, not for following anything that can be worked out by reason or as a project. It is a time for 'allowing' the mysterious energy to flow and permit it to do its work. The work is for purifying the senses and imagination, a time for learning obedience by the things one suffers. Yet, if one only knew the value of each lonely moment, where the sense of being in charge of oneself, which was hitherto taken for granted, is no longer there, moments which grow into hours and days – if one only knew the value of those times one would gladly and willingly accept them and even ask for more.

Another analogy of the Dark Night would be to liken the state to that of a pregnancy. Imagine a woman who was pregnant but who didn't know anything of the facts of what was going to happen to her. She was conscious of differences taking place physically but, as she wasn't aware of what it all meant, she tried to struggle against it and tried to live as she always had, forcing her body to behave as it always had. There was a great struggle that went on for a long time as she tried to cling to things of the past though her body insisted that things were changing. As the time of birth drew near, the pains became so bad that she just had to surrender to it, abandon herself to it all, though in ignorance and in darkness of understanding. She just had to let the process take place. It was not an event that her mind could in any way comprehend, but her body knew how to react and how to allow the forces of nature to take their course.

An account of growth that is happening beneath the surface of consciousness is shown in a passage in Isaiah:

> In your presence, O Lord, we have conceived and been in the pains of labour and have brought forth the spirit of salvation, Is 26:17–18.

Again, this is a description of growth and change taking place at a deeper level than consciousness, a hint, and a sign that 'something' is going to happen that will bring a blessing.

After some time I became aware of the fact that I was now doing some of the things and activities that for so long I had been unable to make decisions about, without a second thought; I was just doing them in an unselfconscious way. It was as if the will-power had regrouped itself round a deeper centre. It is easy to be wise after the event but I now knew it would have been a mistake to try to force myself, even if I could have done, which I couldn't. 'Just let things take their course', I should have said to myself. Perhaps it is akin to St Augustine's saying 'love God and do as you like', or St John of the Cross: 'In darkness and secure, by the secret ladder, disguised'.[7]

> For it has been granted to you, that for the sake of Christ you should not only believe in him, but also suffer for his sake.[8]

> Our basic core of goodness is dynamic and tends to grow of itself. The growing awareness of our true Self, along with the deep sense of spiritual peace and joy, which flow from this experience, balances the psychic pain of the disintegrating and dying of the false self. As the motivating power of the false self diminishes, our true Self builds the *new self* with the motivating force of divine love.[9]

> Then suddenly, when they looked round, they saw no one with them any more but only Jesus.[10]

This is what will happen when the changeover is complete. It means that every person, and every event, will be seen with Jesus at the core of their being. His presence will be recognized within them, so that there will be no judgement or assessment of a person or situation from an outer point of view, but their needs and why they are what they are will be seen from a much deeper level than outward symptoms seem to show. There is an immediacy of being and an ability to let go after the encounter. It is a way of being 'all things to all people' (St Paul).

When the old self creeps back in again, and it does from time to time, it is a mistake to get too downhearted; that could be a sign of false humility. It is better to just go on with hope for the next time. When something happens in outer circumstances that does seem to cause some indecision, it is best to wait and allow the disturbance to settle. For instance when there is some outer indication that God might want something done, or not done, it is still best to wait until the inner conviction becomes the attraction; in the meantime just remain still and constant.

When I came upon this quote from Jan van Ruusbroek,[11] it seemed to sum up and describe exactly the way I should conduct myself. It again speaks of the need for balance which has always seemed so important to me.

> If a person is to be healed of this distress, then they must feel and think that they are not their own possession but that they belong to God. And therefore they must abandon their own self-will to the free will of God, allowing God to act in time and eternity. If they can do this without heaviness of heart and with a free spirit, then at that very moment they will be healed and bring heaven to hell and hell to heaven. For however much the scale of love goes up and down, this person always remains perfectly balanced. For they who suffer without resentment remain free and balanced in their spirit, and they experience the union with God without intermediary.

In this time of purification, cleansing and suffering, we are cleansed at a deeper level than that of our conscious mind. We hang on in faith and 'we learn obedience through the things we suffer' as Jesus did. We have lost our way, or so it seems, and the whole of our purpose in life seems to have got lost. Prayer seems to have disappeared and God is no longer there. This is certainly the time for hanging on in faith and allowing ourselves to be led in unknown ways, ways that are dark and obscure. The reason that it seems that no one can understand our sense of loss is that we 'hear' what they say through the ears of our former way of being, with our earlier structure of values and ways of thinking, whereas those ways are now being taken away from us and are no longer a viable system for assessment.

These new ways now seem dark and obscure because they are quite literally unknown to us, that is, they are at a deeper level than usual consciousness. Until this time we may have thought that our personal identity is in our thinking and reasoning, but those gifts are only tools with which we cope with life as it is presented to us. However, there is more to a human person than just thinking, there is also intuition, which for the Christian, inspired by the Holy Spirit and guided by a foundation based on liturgical teaching, is rooted in our deepest self. It is almost as if we are being taught a new language system at this time, certainly a new set of values.

Prayer can become very painful at times, especially when energies get out of balance due to stress or unresolved difficulties, and hidden tendencies to self-love, which at other times are very peaceful. We learn by way of the pain, what it is that is holding us back and as we begin to correspond to that knowledge, in the dark, light dawns as to what is causing some of the hidden blockages.

As mentioned earlier, our idea of ourselves as a 'person' or a 'persona' seems to be under threat and yet all that has to go. It is like a shedding of an outer covering, rather like a caterpillar feeling restless in its cocoon sensing that it is time to move on, to become transformed but not able to emerge by its own strength or before due time. The very action of emerging from the cocoon is itself strengthening to the butterfly's wings, so it has to wait to emerge at the right time and relying on its own, as yet undiscovered, inner strength, without aid from outer sources.

The gifted times of peace and insight are not only a respite, a station on the way but also a confirmation that the changeover, and transformation is taking place. We can only become our true selves in God. Who that true self is, remains still a stranger to us so we need the Dark Night to bring that real self into our consciousness. When the times of peace come, they are an affirmation that we are beginning to learn something new.

This period can have a very draining and demanding effect physically, due to the reorientation, or changeover in the centre of gravity that is taking place within and there is a need to live quietly and not to be afraid to take rest when needed.

Almighty God you have prepared for those who love you such

good things that pass man's understanding, pour into our hearts such love towards thee that we may obtain unto Thy promises which exceed all that we may desire.[12]

We will sense the need for a greater freedom, an inarticulate desire for a further letting go – letting go into the darkness where lies freedom. If we have had a long history of spiritual direction and yet we cannot now get understanding of this growing new desire to let go into freedom, it can be very painful and challenging. When the need to let go becomes so strong it cannot be resisted, it almost feels like having to choose to face martyrdom rather than to deny the call. Whatever happens it cannot be denied. At that time I had, quite by chance, an encounter with a priest of the Carmelite Order. I said that I had been reading the Carmelite saints for over fifty years and now felt very much aware of a great need to let go of old ways and guidance. Fortunately, he was able to give me welcome confirmation. 'Trust in the Holy Spirit,' he said. It was as if I was launching out into a state of risk, at least that was how it seemed to me, but I had to dare to follow and risk it.

> When people go to the Lord with a firm resolve he never allows them to fall back completely. He sees their weakness and works with them to help. He stretches out his hand of power from on high and draws them to himself. His assistance is at the same time open, yet secret, conscious, yet unconscious, until such time as we have climbed right up the ladder and drawn close to him. Then we will be made one in the All and forget all the things of earth, and be with God, whether in body or out of it I do not know.[13]

The above passage relates to 2 Corinthians 12:2. 'I know a man in Christ who fourteen years ago was caught up to the third heaven. Whether it was in the body or out of the body I do not know – God knows'. (NIV)

> It is only right that our first step should be to take the yoke of Christ's commandments on our shoulders. We should neither kick not drag behind, but go forward in these things straightly and surely until our death.

We should transform ourselves into the new paradise of God until such time as the Son with the Father enters us through the Holy Spirit and dwells within. Then, when we possess him completely as our guest and teacher, he can command any of us, no matter how great the task with which he entrusts us, and we shall simply stretch out our hand to it and accomplish it with all eagerness just as he intended. But it is not right to look for this before the proper time or to accept it from the hands of men. No, we must abide in the commandment of our God and master and wait expectantly for his instructions.[14]

As the Dark Night draws to its close, or at least begins to become more familiar and more comfortable to live with, we may be aware of a need or a call to 'return to the market-place', a return to '*catapheia*' a turning round and giving oneself to whatever comes in an outer sense. This certainly does not mean getting lost in a frenzy of activities but it does mean being ready to respond when outer calls are received. There will now be even more readiness to meet other people and situations as and when they come, exactly where they are, not where we would have liked to think we knew they were. Once this begins, it is likely that even more will be asked as it is outwardly recognized that we have something to offer, something that can be of use. 'Before enlightenment hue wood and draw water, after enlightenment hue wood and draw water'.

If a man cannot feel intuitively[15] that he has put on the image[16] of our heavenly Lord Jesus Christ, man and God, over his rational and intellectual nature, then he remains but flesh and blood. He cannot gain an experience of spiritual glory by means of his reason, just as men who are blind from birth cannot know sunlight by reason alone.[17]

God calls for patience, faithfulness, tolerance and a continuation of the emptying of self. He will take care of all the rest. We stand at the door of our tent waiting to be called to go out like Moses.[18]

CESSATION OF INNER SUFFERINGS

Because we are pilgrims on this earth, from our first cry at birth to our last breath in death we suffer at any stage of prayer growth from the circumstances of human life, weather, weariness, illness, failures and human contradictions. However, as we progress in prayer, we are gradually freed from interior disturbances and sufferings due to sin and imperfection. We recall that the two nights of purification are painful precisely because our selfish clingings are being burned away in the dark fire of contemplative prayer. When this work is finished, there is nothing to be stripped away, nothing to cause inner pain. The person is now purified, and there is consequently no need for further 'working over'. The grinding away is finished. Likewise, there are no distressing longings for the absent Beloved, for the obvious reason that he is now always experienced as present. He no longer withdraws as he did in the spiritual espousals. In place of the aching feeling of emptiness characteristic of the two nights, there is now an abiding and peaceful exchange of love with the indwelling Father, Son and Holy Spirit.[19]

Prayer is not prayer until it becomes something that you *are* rather than something that you *do*.[20]

To pray and live like this means that we shall become, in a sense, almost invisible in the world in which we live, that is to say that we have nothing that is personally distinctive about us, we just adapt and blend into the circumstances and situations in which we find ourselves, that brings a kind of camouflage.

Growing into a Likeness of Christ

There is no commitment that is greater than Baptism: 'I turn to Christ, I repent of my sins, I renounce evil.' To follow this commitment is to follow the way of Transfiguration.

As prayer becomes what it is meant to be, a closer relationship with God, 'something that you *are* rather than something that you *do*',[21] gradually allowing him to take over our lives more and more, together with a gradual letting go of our false selves, the discipline and guidelines that prayer imposes gradually transform us. The transformation only comes about as the false self begins to die. For the surface personality to die seems 'unreasonable and unnecessary' but that is because we have not yet met our own true selves, which lie hidden beneath a persona that has been built up in our early years.

It takes courage to let go of 'oughts'. 'I ought to do this or I ought not to do that', but the criteria should be, 'does it help me grow towards wholeness and integration, towards balance within myself, balance of my own body, mind and spirit and does it help me to be more available and sensitive to God's presence within and so more available for others'. Many people have problems with loving themselves in a good way yet we are asked to love our neighbour as ourselves; so how can we expect to do that if we do not know what it means to care for our own wholeness.

Though I am sure the energies are for the building up of the Body of Christ on Earth, I know that there must be faithfulness in following where I am led without any preplanning of my own. This is not an easy lesson for me to learn as I have a lot of natural enthusiasm and had the ability to plan my life; all that has now to be offered. But I know that it is essential for me to try to be faithful in following the inner disposition of the Holy Spirit and to learn to allow integration of body, mind and spirit to take place.

I now believe more than ever that the purpose of the Christian life is to allow oneself to 'be transformed into a likeness of Christ' as St Seraphim of Sarov would say, 'to acquire the Holy Spirit'.[22] I still believe that the most important and validating aspect of the spiritual life is humility. It is not just a good quality it is a dynamic truth. As I have tried to say earlier that does not mean that we should be afraid to be who we are, in fact it is only by being fully who we are that we can reflect the glory of God.

One of the serious dangers seems to be the temptation to make the mistake of thinking that there are no further roads to travel. Fortunately the long trials of the darker times in prayer soon knock that out quite distinctly. Though it is good to have confidence in one's own vocational pathway. I am thankful too that reading the lives of others' journeys[23] has led me to see that there are always further vistas, which may not necessarily be encountered in this life. I know that it is important to learn to be truly where I am and not to try to be where I am not. The spiritual journey is not a matter of quantity and attainment but of quality and obedience to the Spirit in the present moment.

One of the sorrows of the way is the deep loneliness of not finding many other people with whom I could find empathy or who were on a similar path. In fact there can be an antipathy from some other people who sense at an unconscious level, that there is something different though it is seldom put into words. As Bernadette Roberts says, 'the caterpillars don't always like butterflies even though they themselves were originally destined to become butterflies'. But even that can be accepted and let go of. There really is no need to look sideways at other people who may seem to be in a different place to ourselves.

Intercession

As I have said, the subject of intercession and helping in the work of redemption has always seemed to me to be of great importance and has had meaning for me all through my life. I have long believed that a life of prayer is always a life of intercession, it has to be, whether fully realized or not. It is being to another (inasmuch as one is able, and this is always growing and developing). It is being to another what Christ would be, and in fact is, to them. Being aware of what their need is and where they are in themselves. To come to that place, to see others as Christ sees them is, of course, the work of a lifetime. But it is possible for that growth to be continually developing within us as we grow in our own personal relationship with him. That is the key to a life of intercessory prayer and self-offering – a life of growing personal relationship with the Persons of the Holy Trinity. It all hinges on that. We come to this position by incorporating and accepting our own needs and problems, accepting them together with our prayer, becoming more aware of what our own need is and what our own problems are. We've all got problems but they can be seen as a means of growing and entering more deeply into an understanding of Christ's 'problems', his sufferings – a way of being united with him and so being united with others and just 'being' for them in compassion and love.

It doesn't mean to say that we have to experience all the sufferings that there are, but anything that is in any way a cross for us carries the potential of growth. I remember well a phrase from a sermon given at Fairacres by Fr John Arnson many years ago, 'Walk towards your Cross and it will work for you, pull away from it and it will destroy you'. This is, I think, the crux of the matter, to understand that our own crosses can be a means of life, both for us and for those for whom we pray. I don't mean in a self-conscious way, thinking of reparation or anything like that, just simple love and obedience. Our own particular problems, and you may be thinking of what yours are as you read this, are often just beyond recognition in the depths of our being, but to accept those problems willingly as a means of growing in Christ and alongside Christ is certainly helping in the work of redemption and reconciliation.

> To participate in Christ's reconciliation means to open the whole being to God in all the circumstances of daily life.[24]

This is what we seek to do in our everyday lives, and it is through this that our intercessory life will bring life and grace to those for whom we pray, and not only for those for whom we pray but also for those in whose company we find ourselves albeit the intercessory value is often unselfconscious, and rightly so, but we are being a channel of his love amongst those whom we encounter.

It is important to note that intercession certainly doesn't mean getting emotionally involved with other people's sufferings. That could do more harm than good; we seek to go deeper than that, not so much in a self-conscious way, a way that comes from the mind and personality, but by allowing ourselves to go deeper in prayer, deeper than just personality as we saw in the Dark Night experience, and growth in our own self-knowledge will go alongside the understanding of others; that will be a natural by-product of our own self-knowledge.

I offer another quote from Fr Gilbert Shaw,

> THE HOLY SPIRIT will never give you stuff on a plate – you've got to work for it.
>
> Your work is LISTENING – taking the situation you're in and holding it in courage, not being beaten down by it.
>
> Your work is STANDING – holding things without being deflected by your own desires or the desires of other people round you. Then things work out just through patience. How things alter we don't know, but the situation alters.
>
> There must be dialogue in patience and charity – then something seems to turn up that wasn't there before.
>
> We must take people as they are and where they are – not going too far ahead or too fast for them, but listening to their needs and supporting them in their following. The Holy Spirit brings things new and old out of the treasury.

Intercessors bring the 'deaf and dumb' to Christ, that is their part.
Seek for points of unity and stand on those rather than on principles.
Have patience that refuses to be pushed out; the patience that refuses to be disillusioned.
There must be dialogue – or there will be no development.

The deeper we go in prayer, the closer we get to an understanding of what the cross is for each of us, and how it can bring us towards wholeness. We are all unique and our own crosses are exactly what we need. I once heard Bishop Kallistos say that 'each one of us is an endangered species' there is no one else quite like you and me! Our cross is pruning us for further growth. And through that understanding we can therefore 'be' for other people. If you want to know whether anyone's life is authentically Christian, ask yourself if there is any suffering in that life. If not, it could be just like a lovely picture, glossy and shiny on the outside, but without much depth or meaning within.

I once knew a lady, she is dead now, who said she didn't have any problems – I felt a bit sorry for her.

So that is what Intercession is, 'being', for other people in compassion and love. Certainly not trying to 'do' anything to them or with them; that would be a kind of magic. It is not seeing them from our own point of view, judging and assessing and commenting – being tempted to tell God what they need, or what we think that they ought to have. Some people seem to think that if they keep on long enough, God will give in and give them what we want them to have. Let us remember Psalm 139: 'Thou knowest all my ways and there is not a word on my tongue but that Thou O Lord knowest it long before'. To spend time meditating on that Psalm from another's point of view reminds us that indeed he does know all their needs before we do and that indeed he has plans for them.

Intercession is a looking up to Christ on behalf of others, being a channel of his healing and unconditional love for them. Trusting in his love and in his will. Simply holding them up to God's love. As we make an offering of our own lives, and grow through our own cross, our whole lives become a simple but profound act of intercession for the community, for the church and for the world. As we grow, both in depth of prayer, and through our own problems in company with our Lord, our whole lives are interceding, are becoming one simple single act of intercession. Even as Jesus walked around in the Galilee area, he was redeeming the world and praying to the Father by just being obedient to the duties of his state of life at that time.

It is not so much a matter of *achieving* balance in the whole of our being – that sense of achieving or working to achieve, would speak too much of personality, of will-power – but it is a matter of allowing balance to be wrought in us by the relationship of prayer that we have growing within us.

INDEPENDENT SUSPENSION

> Lions and tigers seem to have independent suspension, as do four-wheel-drive vehicles. They appear to proceed along smoothly enough although in fact they may be travelling over rough terrain. It will be like that for us when we have come to a degree of detachment from the situations and circumstances of our everyday lives.[25]

As we hold and face our own blockages and stand with them, gazing up to the Lord, the process of just standing there changes and transforms us into that channel of his love. As St Francis of Assisi said, 'make me a channel of your peace . . . make me a channel of your love'.

It is a life of love going outward towards the world and other people. Living this kind of intercessory life will certainly benefit us too. Naturally we all have our own personal concerns: family, friends and causes that we want to hold up to God's love, but it is when the whole of life becomes prayer that our intercessions become more effective for the suffering world and that can happen without our even being aware of it.

The psalms get into one's blood stream over the years and familiar verses can pop into one's mind at any time and place. 'Teach me O Lord the way of Thy Commandments and I shall keep them unto the end' ... 'O when shall my ways become so direct that I may keep them forever' (Ps. 119:5). I'm sure that we all have our own favourite and well-known verses. When I fell down some marble steps when I was in Rome and didn't break anything, I remembered 'he shall give his angels charge over thee, they shall bear thee in their hands that thou hurt not thy foot against a stone' (Ps 91). Of course, better people than I have fallen and broken something but I was very thankful at that time.

It is above all good when we can participate in the Office in person, either in church or in the convent, or monastery, but often we have to say the Office alone, or so it seems. But I am persuaded that we are in company with the unseen Church all over the world and maybe with the Angels and the Saints in heaven too.

Naturally we try to have a structure to our lives and our days and to allow a place for the Office, but sometimes, on occasion, we have to let the Church say our share of the Office for us. If we feel called to be connected to an enclosed community, it is to be expected that silence and solitude and times of withdrawal will have some part in our lives, but sometime unforeseen circumstances, duties or health, prevent us from keeping to our usual rhythm. Then we just link in as and when we can, knowing that as we join in when possible, others are still saying the Office when we cannot. We take that patiently, of course, not fretting when we are called to spend our time in a different way. That is what is asked of those called to live the contemplative life in the world, the freedom, flexibility and detachment to adapt to what is asked of us at any given time. It is all a matter of love and obedience to the revealed will of God in the present moment, not rigidity, anxiety or scrupulosity.

A Hermit in Community

To live a life of prayer in the world, hidden and disguised by the ordinariness of our outward appearances and circumstances makes us a 'hermit in community'. Prayer makes our enclosure for us and we are naturally protected from over-involvement with outer things because we have come to know that those things can never give us fulfilment. We sense when to withdraw from, or to be moderate with, outward activity. This is not a discipline imposed by will-power, by our own choice, but an attitude to life that becomes an intuitive response to the call to be silent and to wait on God. There is a sense in which one attains to a great freedom and liberty by not having to rely on outward structures. A hermit in community is not necessarily totally solitary but he/she will have to find their own (idio-rhythmic) rhythm of life, which is always unique for each person and will allow time for solitude, silence, prayer, reading and study. Some manual and creative work is also essential for the unifying of the whole person leading towards unity and balance of body, mind and spirit. That type of work has always been very grounding and unifying, and whole-making for me. Creative or artistic work is indeed good but I know that there could be times when it may be a distraction, depending on the motivation that lies behind the work we do. The Holy Spirit will give the discernment necessary for this creative work, as it is not always easy to know when to let go.

> Prayer is a conversation of the spirit with God. Seek therefore the disposition that the spirit needs, in order to be able to reach out towards its Lord and to hold converse with him without any intermediary.[26]

> When a phrase or a word in a psalm, or in personal prayer, takes hold of our soul or makes the heart exult, we should stop and go deep into this 'intuition of God'. We should cease to multiply words, and find rather the silence in the heart of the word, the Spirit at rest in the Word ... Multiplicity of words from elsewhere of from afar has not that same value as that interior cry,

that sigh perhaps, that betokens the dizzying nearness of the Other.[27]

The aim of a life of prayer is to offer the whole of one's life to God, every moment, not just moments spent in actual prayer time or only in times of formal worship and not to concentrate on becoming excellent at keeping rules but to be faithful in living in the present moment. The hope and aspiration is that as the whole of life becomes simpler it moves towards one single, simple, life of redemptive love and intercession.

A quotation from St Seraphim of Sarov, a Russian Saint who lived in the forests of Divyevo at the end of the 19th century:

God is a fire that warms and kindles the heart and inward parts. Hence, if we feel in our hearts the cold which comes from the devil – for the devil is cold – let us call on the Lord. He will come to warm our hearts with perfect love, not only for Him but also for our neighbor, and the cold of him who hates the good will flee before the heat of His countenance.

And to end, a prayer of someone who was a member of the Dominican Third Order, a tertiary, St Catherine of Siena:

Make me a still place of light,
A still place of love of you,
Your light radiating,
Your love vibrating,
Your truth and your healing
Far flung and near,
To the myriads caught in sickness and darkness,
Lostness and fear:
Make a heart centre here,
Light of the World.

Notes

1. Gregory of Nyssa.
2. J.-P. de Caussade, *Self-Abandonment to Divine Providence*.
3. Jn 12:24–25.
4. Bernadette Roberts, *The Path to No Self*, pp. 9ff.
5. St John of the Cross, *The Ascent of Mount Carmel*, Book 2, chapter 1, stanza 2.
6. Symeon The New Theologian, *The Practical and Theological Chapters*, pp. 66–7.
7. St John of the Cross, *The Ascent of Mount Carmel*, Book 2, chapter 1, stanza 2.
8. Phil. 1:29.
9 Thomas Keating, OSCO, *Open Mind, Open Heart*, p. 129.
10. Mk 9:8 (New Jerusalem Bible).
11. One of the Rhineland mystics of the fourteenth century.
12. Collect for sixth Sunday after Epiphany.
13. Symeon The New Theologian, *The Practical and Theological Chapters*, p. 93.
14. Ibid.
15. Cf. Mt. 15:14.
16. Cf. 1 Cor. 15:49.
17. Symeon The New Theologian, p. 46.
18. Origen, *On Prayer*.
19. Thomas Dubay, SM, *Fire Within*, p. 187.
20. Fr Gilbert Shaw.
21. A quote from Fr Gilbert Shaw.
22. The purpose of the Christian life is the acquisition of the Holy Spirit.
23. Particularly Bernadette Roberts, *The Experience of No Self*.
24. SLG Oblate Rule.
25. My own thought.
26. Evagrius of Pontus on Prayer – [*Philokalia*].
27. Olivier Clément, *The Roots of Christian Mysticism*, p. 201.

Suggested Readings

The Study of Spirituality, edited by Cheslyn Jones, Geoffrey Wainwright and Edward Arnold, SJ. Invaluable as a reference book and resource book.

John of the Cross, Selected Writings, edited by Kieran Kavanaugh, Classics of Western Spirituality Series (Paulist).

The Complete Works of St John of the Cross, edited by Allison Peers.

The Autobiography of St Teresa, The Interior Castle, The Way of Perfection, by St Teresa of Avila. These two writers are unquestionably essential for understanding the way of Christian contemplation.

Self-Abandonment to Divine Providence, by Jean-Pierre de Caussade. Although not written in modern English, it is a very valuable book, at the right time, for learning to 'let go' and let God take control. This book also emphasizes the need to prioritize on the duties of state of life.

The Scale of Perfection, and *Eight Chapters on Perfection and Angels' Song*, by Walter Hilton. He is my favourite of the English Mystics.

The Cloud of Unknowing, translated and edited by Clifton Wolters, Penguin Classics. Another essential book for learning about Christian contemplation. (There are a number of editions of this book available. I use the Penguin edition.)

Revelations of Divine Love, by Julian of Norwich.
Julian was important for me in that she says 'God forgives us, even before we have sinned.

The Fire of Love, by Richard Rolle. This was helpful especially in what he says about 'fire'.

Manual for Interior Souls, by St Francis de Sales. This and
others of the French School were very much of a foundation for me.

Story of a Soul, The Autobiography of St Thérèse of Lisieux.
Very inspiring in simplicity and emphasis on hiddenness.

The Imitation of Christ, by Thomas à Kempis.

The Flame in the Snow, [A Life of St Seraphim of Sarov], by
Julia de Beausobre. An introduction to St Seraphim, to
whom I have great devotion.

The Works of Meister Eckhart (some of these are available in
the Classics of Western Spirituality Series, though other
editions are also available). I find some of Eckhart's writing
rather obscure but was very inspired by his teaching on
detachment, especially as presented in the following books:
The Man from Whom God Hid Nothing, by Ursula Flemming, and
The Way of Paradox, by Cyprian Smith, OSB.

*St Symeon The New Theologian – The Practical and Theolog-
ical Chapters* (Cistercian Publications).

Symeon The New Theologian – Discourses (Classics of
Western Spirituality Series). St Symeon has to be my
favourite Orthodox saint and writer. He is so alive, and his
teaching is just as relevant today as when it was written,
well over a thousand years ago.

Writings from the 'Philokalia' on 'Prayer of the Heart'.
'Presents a specific and coherent view of the Christian life'.
Although I have not read very widely in the *Philokalia,* I
have found much inspiration and support from the work,
particularly from the emphasis that prayer is not only for
monks living in the cloister but for all who seek to practise
'Prayer of the heart'.

St Gregory Palamas and Orthodox Spirituality, by John
Meyendorff.

Any works by St Gregory Palamas. Gregory talks about the
uncreated energies of God and *hesychasm,* which was
helpful to me.

Kundalini Energy and Christian Spirituality, by Phil St Romain.
The first book I read which had a description of 'energies'
that was similar but certainly not identical to my own, written

by a devout Catholic who is a lay minister and a substance abuse counsellor.

The Kundalini Experience, by Dr Lee Sanella. Further information on energies.

The Chasm of Fire, by Irina Tweedie. An explanation of encountering the energies by a woman of the Sufi tradition.

The Path to No Self, by Bernadette Roberts. I found this book very helpful and encouraging in many ways.

The Life of Moses, and *From Glory to Glory* by Gregory of Nyssa. Particularly helpful on the apophatic way.

Any books by William Johnston, SJ. I have read all William Johnston's books and found them all very helpful.

Seeds of Contemplation, and any of the works of Thomas Merton, OCSO.

Open Mind, Open Heart, and *Invitation to Love,* by Thomas Keating, OCSO. All Fr Thomas' books are inspiring with good teaching about the contemplative way.

God Within, and *The Rhineland Mystics,* by Oliver Davies. More on Eckhart and Johannes Tauler; very helpful.

The Beguines, by Fiona Bowey. Very interesting.

Invaded by God, and other titles by George Maloney. George Maloney was a Catholic priest ordained in the Byzantine rite. He is very good on St Symeon, but all his books have that holistic approach that comes with Orthodox teaching.

The Communion of Love, by Matthew the Poor, a Coptic Monk. A book which is entirely God-centred and Gospel-centred, a delight and inspiration.

The Roots of Christian Mysticism, by Olivier Clément. This is an essential book from which to encounter the Orthodox and Oriental aspects of Christian mysticism. It again emphasizes the holistic approach which I find very helpful and inspiring.

Fire Within, by Thomas Dubay, SM. Another favourite book; Fr Thomas brings together the Gospel, St John of the Cross and St Teresa of Avila in an immediate and inspiring style.

Sayings of the Desert Fathers, The Alphabetical Collection, translated by Benedicta Ward, SLG. First published in 1975 by Mowbray's and Cistercian Publications. Revised edition, 1984.

The Way of a Pilgrim, translated by R. M. French.